COLOUR BY

Q·U·A·N·T

MARY QUANT AND
FELICITY GREEN

PREFACE

Colour is what this book is all about. Colour in all its aspects. Its aim — to show you, with a selection of vivid images and simple suggestions, how to look at colour in a new way. How to use it so that it adds to the joy of living.

It will tell you how to choose the colours that suit you best, whatever your colouring, whatever your type. It will advise on colour for your hair and colour for your face. It will show you what colours to wear and what colours to wear with them. It will tell you how and when and where to wear them for maximum impact and style.

Colour is a force to be reckoned with. Every time we buy anything from a pair of panties to a pot of eyeshadow we're drawn in a certain direction by the magnetism of colour. It can affect the way we look but change the mood we're in. It's also a way to have fun, create a stir, break the rules. This book will show you how to make colour work its magic specially for you. It will open your eyes to colour…

I PHOTOGRAPHY STUART MacLEOD
I MAKE UP REGIS HUET

I BEAUTY ILLUSTRATIONS LYNNE ROBINSON
I FASHION ILLUSTRATIONS COLIN BARNES

I COLOUR CONSULTANT URSULA HUDSON

I DESIGN LISA TAI

Colour By Quant was first published
in 1984 by Octopus Books Limited
59 Grosvenor Street
London W1

This special abridged edition
first published 1985

© 1984, 1985 Octopus Books

ISBN 0 86273 232 8

Produced by Mandarin Publishers Ltd
22a Westlands Road, Quarry Bay, Hong Kong

Printed in Hong Kong

CONTENTS

COLOUR YOUR FACE

COLOUR YOUR HAIR

COLOUR YOUR CLOTHES

COLOUR IS LIFE

COLOUR IS PLAYFUL · BLACK IS DEATH
BUT EVEN BLACK PROJECTS LIFE

Masculine fabrics should be in masculine colours — grey, white, black, herringbone, etc., with one romantic lapse of *eau de nil* or *bois de rose*. This perversity delights me but panics the marketing experts who say that it will not sell. But it's wonderful to exaggerate femaleness.

I have a passion for masculine colours and textures — shirtings, pinstripes, Prince of Wales checks, tie-print foulards, pyjama stripes and especially linen, woven in stripes. Linen, covered in creases — and how is it the Italians never sit down?

Colours have changing characteristics — which is why they renew us.

Shocking pink will always be Schiaparelli for me and how I love her for inventing fun, flattery, noise and chic all in one package called 'Shocking'.

It is a smash hit with a tan, golden-red hair and, of course, black.

But Shocking pink has just sneaked up with a new character — call it fuchsia, and wear it with khaki or beige and wow! — knockout sports-chic!

Emerald green has the same virtue and I love it.

Nude pink — that pale, delicate, only-just-pink is very naughty, especially with black. Somehow, it's very difficult to complain about, but it is, of course, downright rude and nude.

Green is having a lovely run; all greens, not just viridian, emerald or forest, but every green under the sun. From bottle green with a greyish tone and looking expensive, to golden delicious, looking noisy and cheap but smart, smart.

Green is new growth, that ruff of pale green that shoots up round the 'dead brown' tree trunks in the streets of Milan.

Later green is the virulent certainty of towels left in the rain at Wimbledon.

Then there is a devilish little green, clear like water colour paint that once was called *eau de nil*. A real balancing trick this one. Two points too strong and the magic has gone — too opaque and too green, it becomes horrid. But it is delicious with terracotta, soft orange and best of all, fawn.

Green needs texture.

Blue is chameleon. Navy blue — hard, cold and officious but navy and white can be deliciously Gigi and Deauville. Gitane blue is pure flattery and Royal blue and black, aggressive Parisien chic with the heart of a whore.

Pale blue is meek, placating and conforming.

White is tennis shoes and blanco.
It's also pristine, white linen longing to be rumpled. But more often now it's drip-dry, crinkled cotton or sweat boiler suits and how I long for my own washing machine and spin dryer in the bathroom. That's luxury.

Red — hard, hot, alive, sure, pushy and crude, blood and guts, cruel, sex, tomato, Spain, rampant, and it always works.

Yellow is smiles, sunshine and scrambled egg and roses, butter and strong confident tractors.

Cream — panama hats, lush warm, texture, rope, string, food, rice, paper, soothing, pearls, silk, pebbles, mornings.

Orange is loud, look-at-me, vulgar. It's alive and awful, rubber and plastic. Orange is optimistic, tough, loutish and lovely.

Brown is warm, renewing and rich. It smells of coffee, toast and chestnuts. The Italians climb into brown leather every winter looking new and confident. Leaving the rest of us looking like tourists or budgerigars.

Beige. One could live forever on greige, beige, fawn, putty and brown paper colour spiked with black, white, conker, chestnut. Then wham in joy with aqua, mauve, *bois de rose*, mahogany, saffron.

Grey is cool and artificially calm. Grey projects other colours. It has a conceited certainty because it does very little to flatter. But dress up grey with gobstopper earrings in yellow or lime. Placate it with white or black and you're away.

PLEASE NOTE, NEVER WEAR ALL BLACK LEATHER WHEN GOING THROUGH CUSTOMS.

Fawn is back. Fawn is a deliciously shifty colour, now beige, now pink, now grey. Fawn used to be silk stockings, cami-knickers and revered dressing gowns. Today fawn looks brand new with pastels or spice colours.

SOME COLOURS NO LONGER REALLY EXIST ALONE BUT WORK IN GROUPS OR SCHOOLS OF COLOUR.

Mary Quant

◆ SCHOOLS OF COLOUR

The pastels are difficult. They quickly look cheap and boring especially when printed on thin white synthetics. On natural fabrics — leather, silk, linen and wool — they look expensive, luxurious and extravagant, because they are!

Pastels are now in fashion every year, but different pastels, differently grouped. Sometimes they are quite fruity, rich tones of melons and roses. Other times, looking new and quite pushy, these are the glacier pastels worn with black, like liquorice allsorts. For grown-up style, add fawn.

The spice colours — yummy spicy sophisticates from hot climes and jungles — khaki, conker, ochre, tabasco, saffron, Pan Yan pickle and tomato chutney.

To be worn by the international saboteurs of conventional good taste, but not to be worried about. They are really very friendly.

COLOUR CAN BE JUST A COMMODITY *OR* IT CAN ADD SPICE. USE IT, EVEN ABUSE IT BUT LOVE IT.

COLOUR

YOUR FACE

Your face is a blank canvas. On it you can paint any picture you like from the subtle to the shocking. And there are plenty of precedents from history, whatever your choice. Cleopatra, just for starters, favoured a bilious green for her eyelids and in Good Queen Bess's golden days, fine blue veins were painted across many a pale and furrowed Tudor brow to give the look of youthful translucence.

Passing lightly through the times when such delicacies as a crocodile's insides or a dollop of cow dung were part of milady's toilette we come to those vapours-prone Victorians who wanted to look pale and interesting and many a prissy miss took to biting her lips, less in anguish than in an attempt to give herself an instant rosebud mouth.

In its time the powder-'n'-paint pendulum has swung its way from one extreme to the other until today when the clever use of make-up is an easily-learnt art-form for anyone who has ever wielded a lipstick. A wondrous palette of vibrant shades will change your ideas and set you thinking about a new, more colourful you. The plan — to make you look prettier, dizzier, crazier, younger, older, sexier — and always aglow with colour.

◆

A SKIN START

In today's world of unlimited colour choices there are no rules and regulations. Conformity is a cop-out rather than a virtue and we can forget all about how we OUGHT to look and concentrate instead on looking our personal and highly individual best. Self-expression is the name of the game and it begins with a bare face. And then the colourful build-up to beauty begins.

It's quite easy, of course, to change the colour of your hair. It's common practice to have pink lips one day and purple the next. Your eyeshadows can be rainbow-bright depending on your fancy and/or the colour of your dress. You could even follow the extreme example of the famous model girl who had a whole wardrobe of contact lenses in all shades from rose red to jade green.

Your skin tone, however, is the skin tone you're born with and remains constant for most of your life save, perhaps, for those few summer sunshine tanning sessions. A peaches-and-cream baby will grow up, lucky thing, into a peaches-and-cream lady and a lily-white lovely will stay lily-white all her life, give or take a tropical holiday or two.

Blends

So your skin tone is where you start to think colourful thoughts and whether you are as pale as a rose petal or dusky as a plum, try to find a foundation identical in tone. And remember that if you're trying and buying in artificial light, the effect will be different in daylight. Liquid, cream, cake or gel, try it out on your neck to see how it blends in with the natural you — or on your face if it's make-up free. Do NOT try it out, as is often advised, on the inside of your wrist. This virgin patch, protected from the elements, is of a totally different tone and texture from your face and neck and will only mislead you into making expensive mistakes. If you have problems finding the right shade, mix two or three different foundations together on the palm of your hand to get just the correct blend.

In general, skin tones break down into three groups: the pinks, the peaches and the black or dusky shades. We all belong to one or the other. . . .

◀ Pallid is a prettier way of saying sallow. A pallid skin that lacks colour needs warm beige to bring it to life and make it less yellow. From then on the choice is wide open for a whole host of glowing lip and eye colours.

▼ Lily white may be lovely but it may also be in need of a touch of extra colour for a healthy-looking glow. The best choice — and don't forget to blend in under the jawline — is a pale natural shade with the merest touch of translucent pink.

◄ The typical English rose — the peaches-and-cream girl who glows from within. Her radiant natural colouring is basically in the golden group so she must beware of any foundation with too much underlying pink.

▼ A dark and dusky skin tone, whether it's blue-black or palest coffee, will always look its best with the highlights of a healthy sheen. Use a special cover-stick to disguise differences of pigmentation.

◄ No, Oriental skin isn't always yellow in tone. It can be as pink as an English rose or a Japanese cherry, but is always delicate in effect. So keep foundation light in texture as well as tone. Emphasise Oriental eyes with pinky brown and lavender shadows blended over the lid to the outer corners.

▶ She's the girl with the built-in blush and her cheeks, provided they're not TOO rosy, give her that enviable glow. Her look is essentially outdoorsy and all the undertones in her fresh complexion are clearly pink. If the glow is a shade too much, cover up with a foundation one tone lighter.

▲ The Asian skin is often pallid and surprisingly peach in tone. It can come prettily to life with a tawny-toned foundation that gives the skin a sheen and provides the perfect foil for exotic eye make-up and decoration.

▲ In days gone by freckles were considered to be a liability. Now they are a definite asset. To make the most of them apply the lightest, most translucent foundation that lets the freckles show through.

► Olive skin is a contradiction in terms: it's not fair and it's not dark. It's without a trace of pink and yet it's not basically yellow. It's an attractive hybrid that looks its dramatic best in the deep beige tones that bring it to warm life.

BASIC BUILD-UP

What should a foundation actually do? That's right — it should lay down a good foundation on which all other effects depend. Its main function is to remove all visual changes of tone: to provide you, the artist, with a primed canvas on which to create a colour picture of you at your brilliant best. First, as everyone knows, you must cleanse, tone and moisturise according skin type and that this should be done night and morning. Now, from the wide choice available, choose the foundation that's right not only for your skin tone but also its type.

The lightest cover comes from the tinted *liquid* foundations, usually with a built-in moisturiser. There are also water-based liquids for oily skins. You'll get slightly heavier cover from the 'whipped cream' kind. The cake make-ups need to be applied with a sponge, give good cover but tend to be drying. In the summer — or even at other times if you'd rather look bonny than pale and interesting — the clear gels and tinted glossers will provide colour without cover.

But to wipe out any real blotches, blemishes or minor birth marks you can't beat the cake or stick solid colour that you apply — gently please — with your fingertips, blending in as you go.

For a really strong cover-up job the cake or stick types do work best. Whether you use your fingers or a small natural or synthetic sponge to apply your foundation don't forget to check that perfection doesn't stop at chin level. Your neck is part of the picture too, and so are your eyelids. Before the foundation is finished you need the artful aid of the real deceivers — the pencils, stick or wands in skin tones that are vital to blot out any tell-tale darker patches that peep through even the most opaque foundations. Some make-up experts advise using these cover-ups under the foundation, some suggest using them last. Test both to see which suits your skin best but don't forget — you're working towards a one-tone overall effect. No blotches, no variations in pigmentation. A monotone perfection is your aim . . .

► If your skin starts out perfect, congratulations! If not disguise the flaws with a special cover-up. Choose the foundation tone closest to your own to blot out shadows and gradations of colour under the eyes (a); in the eye sockets (b); around the nose (c); and down to the corners of the mouth (d). Dot or stipple on where required and use your fourth finger to blend in.

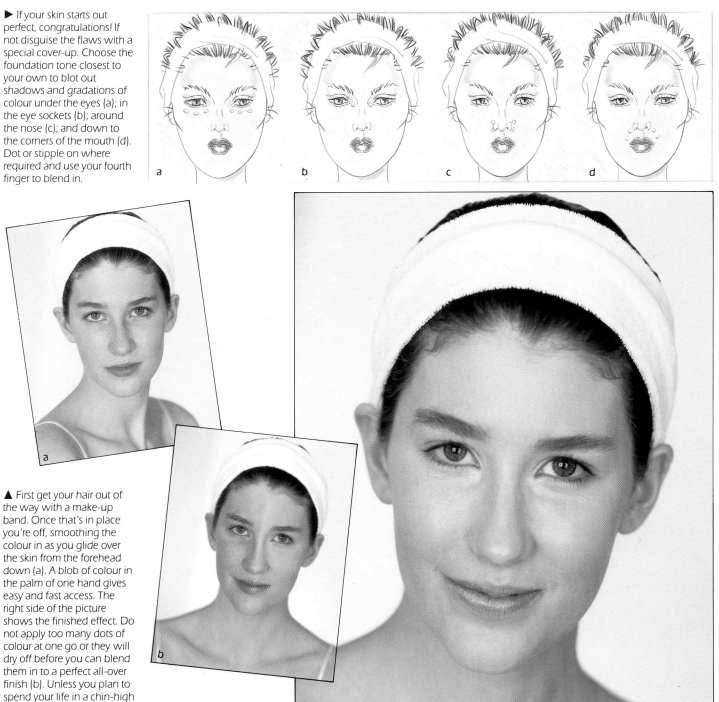

▲ First get your hair out of the way with a make-up band. Once that's in place you're off, smoothing the colour in as you glide over the skin from the forehead down (a). A blob of colour in the palm of one hand gives easy and fast access. The right side of the picture shows the finished effect. Do not apply too many dots of colour at one go or they will dry off before you can blend them in to a perfect all-over finish (b). Unless you plan to spend your life in a chin-high polo sweater, your neck needs the same loving care (c).

PICK YOUR POWDER

The foundation is in place and it looks good so why do you need to powder at all? Because without powder's stabilising influence all the magical colours yet to come would blotch and 'bleed' and the picture you are building up, step by colourful step, would be out of focus in no time at all. Powder is the 'fix' that keeps your face in place whatever your skin type. It will transform the shine of the foundation into a much more subtle sheen. The eyeshadows, the blushers, the highlights — they all need a powder base of one kind or another on which to perform their magic.

The first powders to adorn the feminine faces of the 20th century tended to be chalk white and were meant to show. Today the available colours range from the same baby talk white right up to deep mahogany. Most powders whatever their colour are translucent which means that having imparted their sheen to the skin they virtually disappear. Then there are the irridescent powders, some of which contain particles of ground pearls or fish scales to give them an inbuilt glitter which could be mistaken for tiny sweat droplets, and are considered very desirable in the exercise-conscious '80s. Some of these glisteners are terracotta-coloured but brushed on to the skin, they all but disappear leaving only a healthy glow.

Your first choice depends on the texture you prefer and it's between the loose and the compressed kind. Loose powder which gives a light but matt finish should be applied with a fluffy puff (scrupulously clean, of course) or, if you prefer them, cotton wool balls or a huge powder brush. Apply very generously over the face and neck. Then take a complexion brush and use it in circular motions to remove excess powder, especially in the crevices. If you prefer compressed powder, which gives a denser cover to all kinds of skin types, then use a flat puff to dab it firmly on to the skin. Whatever you do, don't rub or scrub or it will blend into your foundation and make a veritable pudding. And if you reapply compressed powder too often during the day you will turn it into another culinary disaster — a layer cake.

▶ Allow a few minutes for your foundation to dry before you start to powder (a).
Using a flat or fluffy puff, or pieces of cotton wool, blend the powder into the skin from the forehead down (b). Never rub or even stroke. Now take a complexion brush and whisk away the excess powder from every crevice (c).
Result: a matt bloom that's ready and waiting for the next exciting step (d).

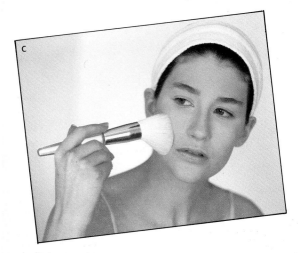

SHAPING UP

Once upon a time if you had a face that was too long/fat/round/square, all you could do was gloom. Now you can reach for the shaders and the shapers in tones from deepest terracotta to palest pearl to give yourself the contours that nature overlooked. The darker shades retreat, the paler ones advance. A highlight here, a lowlight there and the square is rounded off, the round is slimmed down, the heart-shape looks less triangular and the perfect oval looks even more so.

Most shaders and shapers are in compressed powder form and should be applied over the powdered face with a generous complexion brush. For very dry skin use the cream type under your powder. Used with restraint, a hint of colour on the nose makes you glow with health. Take the colour up to your temples and, again, it adds a look of vitality.

Heart

Long

Square

Round

Oval

▲ Shaders and shapers can deceive the eye, create illusions, add interest. They can accentuate the positive and help to eliminate the negative.
Check your face shape against the types shown here and use a light shaper (highlighted) and a dark shader to chart your colour course towards the perfect oval. The left-hand side of the face shows how much of each and where to apply. The right-hand side shows the effect once the colours have been blended into the skin. Most shaders and shapers look darker in their containers than they will on your skin.

TOUCH OF BLUSH

Once upon a time it was simply called rouge and it was used to give instant and unnaturally red cheeks to otherwise sickly-looking ladies. Now it's called a blusher and it comes in all colours from earth brown to purple grape. But even if the colours themselves are bold, the technique for applying them to the best advantage requires a deft hand with the complexion brush since the blusher is the final finishing touch before the eyes and lips receive their shade of colourful attention. For the best effect use at least two complementary tones, stroking them on.

Like the shapers and the shaders, which are already in place, the blusher is used to provide not only colour but also contour so it's not only what you wear that matters but also where you wear it. A strategically placed blusher can take you a long way towards that perfect oval.

Long

Square

Round

Oval

Heart

▲ Which shape is you? The heart, the long, the square, the round or, lucky you, the perfect oval. Check your face against the types shown here and apply preferably two complementary colours as and where indicated on the left side of the drawings, the dominant colour in the middle, the secondary colour more lightly applied above and below. Use a brush to stroke on and then blend them in with your fingertips to give the effect shown on the right side of the face. Go gently though . . . it mustn't disappear and even the darkest shaders and shapers tend to 'fly' during the day.

MAKING EYES

Making eyes used to mean sending out sexy signals . . . and come to think of it, what's new? Eye make-up today is as seductive as it has ever been, including the time when those alluring ladies from Ancient Egypt got the whole beauty business off to such a galloping start with their kohl-ringed eyes. Kohl, we are told, was made from such exoticisms as burnt almonds and brown ochre mixed with animal fat, vegetable oil or . . . saliva. So using spit to apply your mascara may not be ladylike but there *are* precedents.

Through the ages those well-named windows of the soul have been annointed with colours ranging from the subtly natural to the outrageously obvious until today when there is a seemingly infinite number of wondrous shades from which to choose and nothing from acid yellow to pomegranate pink is out of order. What is *in* order is to use a minimum of two colours, and three or four or even more are even better. To work their maximum colour magic they have to be blended together with all the care and expertise that ensures a perfect finish. And we all know what makes perfect: it's practice.

Colours galore, gorgeous colours, and

you're about to make your choice. Hard and fast rules? None exists and if a colour takes your fancy, then follow where your fancy leads. But if a guideline or three wouldn't go amiss among all those seductive shades then consider the colour of your eyes, the colours you like to wear and the time of the year.

If you're a blue-eyed beauty then by all means have blue in your make-up box but don't have *only* blue. The same goes for brown, grey, hazel or green eyes. Contrasts are more fun than the perfect match. If you're wearing a particular dress in a particular colour for a particular occasion and it's bright royal blue, then choose shadows in all the blues from baby to navy with, perhaps, a pearl highlight of which more later.

Finally, just as you wear different clothes for different seasons, why not do your face the same flattering flavour?

THE RIGHT KIT

The colours, of course, come first and are used to accentuate the contours of the eye. But it's skill you need to make them work their magic. Applying eye make-up so that it looks both subtle and sensational is far from a cinch . . . something you do with ease the first time you try it. It's every bit as tricky as making a soufflé or learning to drive and you may well hang on to your L-plates for quite a while. So if at first you don't succeed, etc., etc. You certainly will NOT succeed unless you have the right equipment and your mascara plus your middle finger really won't do. You will need a fine brush to draw the line behind the top lashes, broad brushes to apply colour, soft coloured pencils if you prefer them to cream or powder shadows, highlighters in liquid, powder or stick form and a brisk little brush to get the gunge out from your eyebrows. You will need a pair of tweezers for errant hairs and eyelash curlers for straight ones. Mascara can be either liquid with its wand applicator or in block form with its own little brush. Don't, whatever you do, tilt your head back when you're applying all those lovely shadows or you'll find them all in the wrong place when you straighten up . . .

Final word of warning: most of today's eye cosmetics are made to last. Some are even waterproof. If you try to scrub them off at the end of the day you will wake up in the morning looking like a panda. Use one of the specially formulated liquids or pads. If you choose the liquid, a drop the size of a pinhead is sufficient.

▶ The eyes have it . . . whether brown, blue *and* green . . . To make up, begin at the beginning with foundation over the lid. Allow to dry. A touch of powder to 'fix', a twist of the curler and the colour magic begins. First the lid in one colour and then the socket in another. Brush with a soft foam applicator and blend in with a finger if necessary (a). Next a fine line behind the lashes using either a pencil or a brush and another beneath the lower lashes (b) and (c). Then mascara . . . a moment to dry . . . then more mascara (d).

a

b

c

d

▶ There are plain colours and there are pearlised ones (best on younger, smoother eyes). There are pale colours and bright ones. Blended together they provide endless opportunities for special effects. Dark shades 'retreat', light ones 'advance' so use them to give contour as well as colour, to correct any bad points and emphasise all those good ones.

▲ **Small eyes** look less so with a soft stroke of colour used under the bottom lashes as well as on the lid. Avoid using too much black mascara.

▲ **Close-set eyes** will be drawn apart and look prettier with shadow that is at its lightest near the nose, darkening out towards the outer corners.

▲ **Wide-set eyes** will look their best with colour blended in to the inner corners to bring them a fraction closer to-gether.

▲ **Deep-set eyes** will 'advance' with pale colours blended across the lid. Coloured mascara — dark blue or purple — will be more flattering than black.

▲ **Protruding eyes** need lots of colour above the eye as well as below it. 'Smudge' the colours to soften their effect with a soft brush or a finger.

A LOOK AT LIPS

The word stick as in lipstick is almost a misnomer. Apart from lipsticks there are now lip pencils, lip paints and lip glosses. There is also a white cream fixative which used as an undercoat will keep your chosen colour in its place longer and better. To apply lip colour so that it looks as good as it can and stays as long as it should, you need a small but vital equipment kit.

You will need a fine lipbrush to draw in the outline — or, if you prefer them, lip pencils in shades one or two tones darker than the main lip colour. To keep these pencils in fine shape you will need a special pencil sharpener. (They work better if you pop the pencil in the fridge for half an hour before sharpening.) To fill in the colour you will need another thicker pencil or a flat-tipped lip brush. Make sure there is a layer of foundation on the lips before you start. If you suffer from dry lips, chapped lips or you tend to chew or lick off the colour, invest in one of the new cream preparations that not only 'fix' the colour but also moisturise. Apply this not only over the lips themselves but also on to the skin area around the mouth — this will stop the colour 'bleeding'. Then draw in your outline. Fill in and press hard on a tissue. Outline again, fill in again and press again. Optional extra: a touch of gloss if you want to shine. If you need a re-paint job during the day or evening, try to remove the residue before beginning. And don't forget to start with a layer of foundation so keep a small container tucked away in your handbag for this purpose.

▶ First the outline (a) using a finely sharpened lip pencil. Then the fill-in (b) using a special square-ended lip brush saturated with lipstick. And then, if you like the high-shine look, the touch of gloss (c). There are transparent colours specially produced to give this slightly 'gooey' effect, beloved of sultry sex symbols. If you have a tendency to turn lip colours blue this is due to acid in the system so choose tawny or peachy tones rather than the pinks or wine reds.

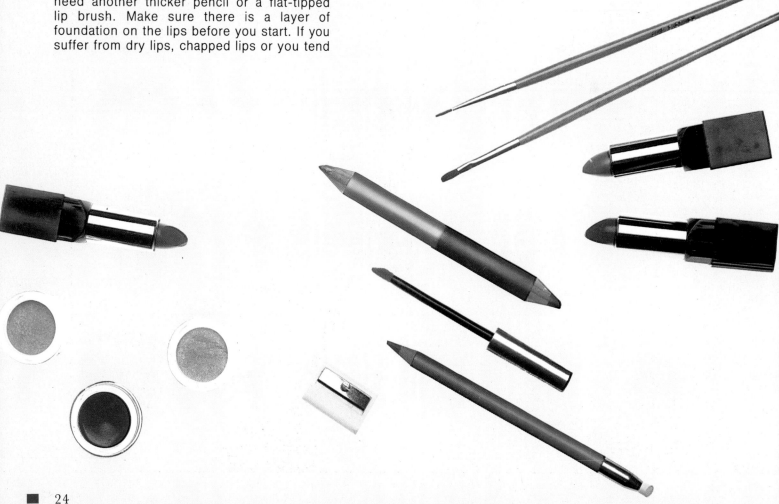

FINGER TIPS

Elegant slender hands with perfect ovals at the tip of each tapering finger . . . This is the stuff of dreams and/or genes.

Happily for most of us there is a great deal that can be done to improve on nature if what we're born with is less than perfect. Every time you wet your hands, dry them *thoroughly* — damp hands get dehydrated. And use a hand cream. If you can bear rubber gloves use them for all your dirty deeds, especially for gardening. If you can't bear gloves, then use a special barrier cream or the effort to scrub nails clean will guarantee future breakages. One famous hand model goes to bed every night in rubber gloves which she wears over cotton gloves which have been soaked in hand lotion. She has wonderful hands. She lives alone. For the rest of us there are less drastic ways to look after our most often exposed extremities.

Contrary to popular belief, what you eat has no effect on the nails — what does affect them is tender loving care. And frequent manicures for which you need just the minimum of equipment. Orange stick, emery board, cuticle clippers, a cuticle solvent and some cotton wool will see you off to a splendid start.

▶ With time to spare and a party to go to, experiment with different colours and different patterns. This spot and geometric effect was achieved with an accurate eye, a steady hand and a colour 'plan' carefully worked out in advance . . . plus plenty of time and patience.

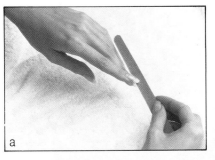

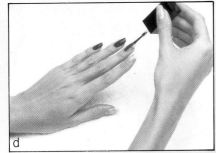

◀ A treat for your hands — the DIY manicure. Remove old polish and file BEFORE you soak, using an emery board in a one-way motion from the side to centre (a). Using cuticle clippers, gently trim off any hang nails. Using your thumb, cream round the cuticle and push gently back (b). Wash but do not leave too long in soak (c). Apply a clear basecoat to prevent discoloration. Now comes the colour, applied in smooth, fast strokes from cuticle to tip (d). Allow to dry and then reapply. The finishing touch — a clear protective top coat which should be reapplied every other day or so.

A FOOT AHEAD

Did you know that Victorian ladies were not allowed to refer to their aching feet? They could say their right foot ached and their left one also but feet in the plural were unmentionable in polite society. Today no one has such fetishes and how to keep your feet looking good and feeling fine is well worth talking about. And DOING something about. Happy feet start with a once-a-month pedicure and will continue to look and feel their best with a constant daily care routine. Use a pumice stone to keep hard skin at bay, and every time you smooth on your body lotion after the bath, spread it right down to your heels and between your toes. To keep your nails in shape use curved clippers rather than scissors but always cut them straight across, just level with the top of the toe. And do use varnish on your toenails all year round rather than just in the summer months when it's maximum exposure time. Brightly painted toes make a cheering sight at the end of the bath as you begin each working day. Whenever you can, be a barefoot girl. Feet benefit from the extra freedom and mobility just like the rest of us.

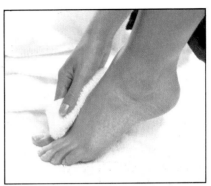

◀ Start with a wash — a few drops of shampoo in the sink if you're supple or a bowl if you're not. Scrub the toenails with a soft brush. Dry and, using your towel, gently push the cuticles back. Now apply a cuticle cream, massaging it well into the nailbed. Use your fingers for this or an orange stick wrapped in cotton wool.

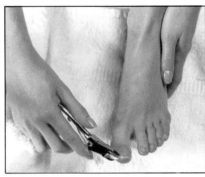

◀ To avoid ingrowing at the corners, toe nails should always be cut straight across. Smooth off any sharp or rough edges with the coarse side of an emery board. Then, using an orange stick, clean out any 'debris' from under the nail. Do not use a file or metal instrument for this as it can cause damage.

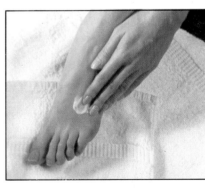

◀ Feet are in constant need of the friendly caress of your handcream or body lotion. Gently pull each toe as you massage it in and pay special attention to any rough patches on the heel. Half a cut lemon will also work wonders on any 'cheese grater' skin. If your feet get hot, dab with surgical spirit and then talc.

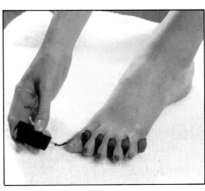

◀ All but the most perfect toes overlap a touch so keep them apart and your paintwork intact with rolled-up pieces of tissue or special sponge separators available from most chemists. Apply a colourless basecoat, then two coats of colour and then a topcoat. Allow at least 20 minutes to dry or you'll have to start all over again!

PARTY FACES

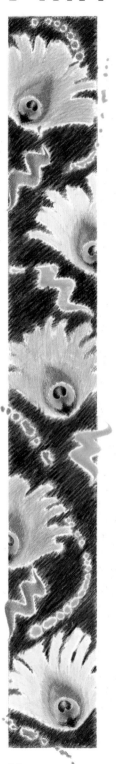

Party dresses. Party faces. We live in a world of wonderful, colourful fantasies so throw restraint out of the window — at least until the morning after — and try your hand at painting on a party face.

Using coloured crayons, start with a sketch carefully worked out in advance on paper. When you have an idea that pleases, draw the basic outlines lightly on to your skin before attempting to block in with solid col-our. Use water-based colour for easy removal and have at least one dummy run until you're reasonably confident It Will Be All Right On The Night.

Ideas to start you thinking: glitter dust, stick on gold or silver stars, sequins, rhinestones. Your face awaits . . . What you need before you start: a small sponge or two, a selection of brushes, a steady hand . . . and a spirit of adventure.

▼ Two fabulous fantasies to inspire you!
Left, a romantic froth of cream, yellow and vibrant pink.
Right, sheer drama contoured in black and white with a flash of gold on the brow and a metallic golden mouth to match. So start practising right now . . .

SPRING SURPRISES

Spring has sprung and it's up to you to do likewise. Spring is the time to behave like a tree, a flower, a young man's fancy. Break into bud (all shades of green golden tones), burst into bloom (all shades of pink and/or gold) or, like the aforementioned young man, let your fancy rise to the occasion. Of all the seasons that supplant one another in our scheme of things, spring is the time for a total re-think, a time for experiment. Lips that have been wine dark for winter can sing out in orange, pumpkin or petal pink. If winter has left you pale and wan, lighten and heighten the outlook with warm toffee or rosy blushers. Shade your eyes with a combo of green, pink and gold. Be daring, be bold-... to use the same colours in March as you use in November is a crime against Nature and you're not doing yourself much good either. Take your lead from what you see. If Dayglo is the season's favourite fashion ·shade, then have a go with Glo. It's pale and fragile apple blossom pink? Then you, too, should blossom forth. And never say never when choosing colours for the New You. Lovely surprises could be in store as you open up a new palette of untried tones, especially if you start with an exfoliating facial to slough off the old winter-worn skin along with your cocoon of heavy winter clothes. This way you give your face a colourful head start . . .

SUMMER SIZZLERS

Summer is a cumin' in and with it come all the lovely, lush colours that glow warmly against a tanned skin . . . the colours of soft summer fruits and fragile summer flowers — the hot pinks, the glowing peaches, the rosy reds, the leafy greens and the clear blues of a cloudless summer sky. Summer is the time to experiment with paintbox pastels which suddenly come alive against a golden tan. But is that tan really real or artfully artificial? If you're wise it's definitely the latter. A sunburn is just what it says it is and those pale beauties of the past who never ventured out without their parasol knew a thing or two about the effects of ultra-violet on their fragile epidermis. It not only darkened it, it thickened it too. Today, of course, we're much more sensible: we take our sunshine in very small doses and top up our tans from a bottle, spray or tube. Wondrous, glowing-with-health looks can be ours in an instant with none of the hazards — or the sweat — of the real thing. There are mousses and creams that colour the skin and stay convincingly in their place for days on end. Then there are see-through gels that bronze and moisturise and disappear overnight, cleansed away like a good cosmetic should be. What a summer skin does not need to look is matt. A slight sheen, a high temperature 'hot' look makes the perfect foil to the light, clear lip and eye colours that look their best under the summer sun.

AUDACIOUS AUTUMN

Suddenly it's NOT summer. The delicate tan you've been nursing along now looks a faded yellow and at the fall of a leaf it's time to move forward a season. To autumn. To a succession of clear, cool days when there's a nip in the air and a glow on the cheeks. Suddenly we're into the season that is full of rich, vibrant UNEXPECTED colours. All tones of wine are wonderful for autumn both for the lips and eyes. So are deep greens, aubergine, grape and the dark wine reds of the late berries. Claret and lavender work particularly well together to get us from summer's naive sunshine shades into the subfusc subtleties of hazy autumn days. These then are the autumn colours for lips, for eyes, for cheeks, for shadows and for fingernails. But make-up shades should always be selected to work together with the colours that are fashion's current favourite. If fashion indicates that Brown is Big, then you can be sure that the beauty business will be telling the same story. In fact, cosmetic colours today have less to do with the face and more to do with fashion. Once upon a time lips were red as rubies, eyes were dark as pansies and teeth were white as pearls. Always. In today's wonderful free-for-all colour fantasy, eyes can be shadowed in ruby red and lips can be painted pansy dark. Teeth, at this moment in time, tend still to be white as pearls. But who knows for how long . . .?

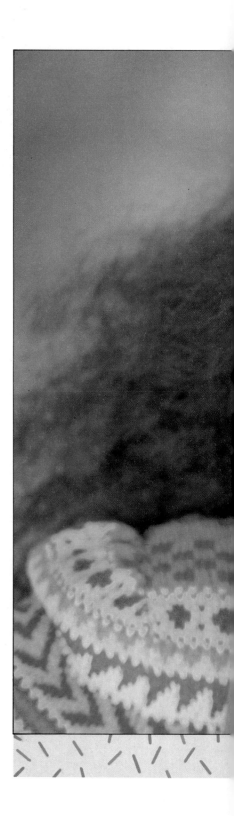

WINTER WONDERLAND

Every season has its special appeal. Spring is an invitation. Summer is a consummation. Autumn is a rejuvenation. And winter is a real challenge. Unkind winds do their blustery worst to blow away that inner glow and the common cold is the common enemy so our make-up must take over where nature leaves off. It's the time of the year to use colour with a free and bold hand, no coincidence that each winter season we are presented with a rich and vibrant palette of cosmetics created to provide a lively contrast to the basic colours in our winter wardrobe. The sombre grey, black, brown or wine of winter all need a little help from their friends — the vivid lip colours, the sizzling eye shadows, the warm-toned blushers. Now, more than at any other time, there's the need to experiment with really vivid effects. If you've never worn a poppy or ruby red lipstick, do it now. Try out pink, blue, green or lavender eyeshadow. Or all four blended together. Go for a touch of golden frost mingled with russet. And try out coloured mascara, dark green, lavender or chocolate. If nature hasn't provided you with a built-in rosy glow, do it yourself with a cream blusher applied over the foundation and under translucent powder. Again it's a time for being definite so choose rosy, lively shades rather than the pallid pinks. Gently brush off the excess powder and you should look a picture of health.

COLOUR
YOUR HAIR

Not for nothing has it been called our crowning glory. But just supposing that the particular crown bestowed on us by nature is in a shade we don't altogether fancy, what exactly can we do about it? In days long gone, very little used to be the case. Other than fret. Or bleach. Or dye. Brunettes who'd rather be a blonde reached for the peroxide bottle, mousy or grey-haired types went boot-black and natural blondes rejoiced in the belief that Gentleman Preferred Them. (Even then, some did and some didn't.) To colour your hair in those drastic days was a distinctly dicey business. Not only was there the risk of being thought 'fast', but sometimes your hair fell out. Today, thanks to the combination of inspiration and technology the dice are loaded in our favour and a wide and wonderful world of hair colour awaits anyone who is less than delighted to be as dark/light/mousy or carrotty as she started out. Hair that's damaged, wispy, greasy or just plain dull can benefit from the current coupling of colourants and conditioners. The right product carefully chosen to do the right job can work wonders, transforming even the legendary English mouse into the flame-haired temptress she always longed to be. But which product in what colour? New readers start here . . .

41

KNOW YOUR TYPE

There are different kinds of colouring for different kinds of hair, each designed to do a different job. Some last for one shampoo, some for five or six, some stay around until that half-an-inch-a-month regrowth exposes the Before and After. Some are whole-head, whole-hog effects with dramatic colour changes that require a completely new make-up to say nothing of a change of wardrobe. Some rely more subtly on a mere change of tone. Some make you lighter and some make you darker. Some offer attractive two-, three- or even four-tone effects with combinations of highlights and lowlights. Millions of dollars have been spent in recent years by the leading manufacturers of hair colourants in order to make them not only attractive and efficient but also foolproof — and yes, they do mean most of us.

In order for each product to work its maximum magic it has to start on healthy hair. Badly bleached, perm-damaged or generally out-of-condition hair will not give colour a chance. Hair belongs to one of four categories and each type responds to different tender loving care. There's a lot that can and should be done to bring your hair up to tip-top condition before you finally take that quantum leap into the wide and wonderful world of colour that awaits.

◀ Does she or doesn't she? In days gone by the blonde in question wasn't telling if she did or didn't. Today she more often does and it's no longer easy to spot whether the blonde is for real or out of a bottle.

▲ Take one head of rich newly brown hair in mint condition and combine it with a zippy young layered style. The result: a perfect marriage between sharp shape and glowing colour.

Is your hair oily, dry, mixed or normal? What we all want, of course, is to be normal with malleable tresses that respond amiably with a minimum of fuss. Few of us, alas, lead such a trouble-free life. But whatever your problem, there's a lot you can do to correct it and most of it happens at shampoo time.

IF YOUR HAIR IS OILY don't listen, whatever you do, to old wives' tales that warn about washing only making it worse. It can't and it doesn't. Maybe it did when we used to wash our hair in carbolic soap. Today's shampoos are a different kettle of gentle unguents. Oily hair starts with an oily scalp which often starts with eating all the wrong things. So concentrate on fresh fruit and vegetables and cut out the fatty, sticky horrors. Shampoo frequently — daily if possible — but use a 'frequent use shampoo' and go easy with the scalp massage. Use a conditioner only on the ends. And cut out the vigorous brushing those same old wives were so keen on. This just stimulates the sebaceous glands in the scalp and spreads the trouble too far too fast.

IF YOUR HAIR IS DRY you must be doing something wrong. Over-bleaching? Over-perming? A blow-dryer too hot or heated rollers used too often? To give the hair a good head start, shampoo frequently with a mild shampoo, one application only, massage the scalp and apply a cream conditioner as often as required. Use a wide-toothed comb rather than a brush to style it into place. Let it dry naturally as hot air from a dryer will exacerbate the dryness. If your scalp is flaky it does not necessarily mean you have the dreaded dandruff. A fingertip massage once a week with warmed almond oil can bring about a minor miracle. You'll need two shampoos to remove. Also excellent — intensive care treatments every couple of weeks.

IF YOUR HAIR IS MIXED this is because the sebum glands get blocked at scalp level. Result: greasy scalp, dry hair. In this worst of all possible worlds you *must* shampoo frequently, gently massaging your scalp with your fingertips. Use a conditioner on the ends only and style with a coarse comb.

NORMAL HAIR? Congratulations!

TAKE YOUR PICK

The decision is made and the dye, if you will pardon the expression, is cast. Like millions of women before you and the millions still to come you are going to change the colour of your hair. Unlike your predecessors, however, you do not reach for the leeches, ashes or goat's fat. Your basic reasons, however, are probably the same. We colour our hair in order to follow fashion, improve the 'nondescript', add texture and body, give our spirits a lift, make us look more smart/glamorous/sexy/younger, disguise tell-tale grey. In order to achieve the infinite variety of effects there is now an infinite variety of products. (One firm alone offers more than 200 different tempting colours.) The choice is nothing short of bewildering.

What's Best?

How do you pick the one that's best for your hair and most likely to provide the effect you want? Do you want to experiment short term — put your toe in the water rather than plunge in at the deep end? If so, the world of the water rinse, gel, mousse and spray is your oyster. These all wash, or, in the case of the spray, just brush out and you're back to basic in minutes. For something longer-lasting but not irrevocable there are the semi-permanent rinses that last through four to six shampoos. (Here today and gone the day-after-the-day-after-tomorrow if you shampoo as often as you should.) For those in search of a drastic change there are the long-lasting dyes and tints that are there until re-growth at the rate of about half-an-inch a month catches up with them.

Basically there are eight different colourful routes to follow. Some take time, some take courage, some work better on one type of hair than on another, some need an expert hairdresser to apply. Study the chart on the right carefully, take your own hair and its current condition into account and off you go.

Final words of wisdom from the experts: more grief is caused by not reading the instructions TWICE than by picking the wrong shade. And in general it's more flattering to go lighter than darker.

WHAT KIND OF COLOURING . . . ?	BEST USED ON WHAT TYPE AND COLOUR OF HAIR . . . ?	HOME	SALON
Water Rinses That merely give the hair a colour 'over-coat'	All types but best on light or mousy or greying hair	●	●
Semi-Permanent Rinses This penetrates the hair's outer 'cuticle' giving extra depth and richness to the original shade	All types — and again best on the mid-brown to fair shades	●	●
Permanent Colour A dye by any other name . . .	All types, all colours, no holds barred but expert advice is a good idea if the change is a drastic one	●	
Spray-on Colour Today's way to get weird shafts of light and shade at the press of a button. Often metallic	All types/all colours depending on the degree of impact required	●	●
High, low and inbetween lights A mixture of shades often called by fancy names — the gun, streaking, flashing, tipping etc	All types but adds interest and drama to mousy blondes or dull brunettes	●	●
Henna Popular since ancient times and the only 'natural' colour still in popular use. Also available as a chemical	All types but best on dark or very dark hair. Blondes and grey heads beware — can be carrotty	●	●
Mousse Varies from instant one-shampoo colour to semi-permanent; conditions as well as colours	All hair but most effective on the lighter shades	●	●
Gel Like an old fashioned brilliantine but non-greasy	Best when wet. Most effective on fair hair — 12 shades available from Old Gold to Metallic Red	●	●

WHAT'S THE EFFECT?	HOW LONG DOES IT LAST . . . ?	HOW IS IT USED?
Depends on the original hair colour and the shade chosen; light hair will react more noticeably than dark	Just until the next shampoo	After shampooing, but the instructions will vary from product to product. Read first and inwardly digest
Refreshes and enlivens existing colour. Particularly kind to greying hair as the contrast will be gentle	Between 4 to 6 shampoos — the effect will fade gradually, wash by wash	Again, read the instructions carefully for specific do's and don'ts — takes about 30 minutes to set so don't be in a rush
Can be a complete made-over job including stripping down and covering-up. Also used for 'patches' of contrast colour	Till the roots demand a retouch — or you change your mind	Extremely carefully! And an allergy and colour test are strongly advised
Startling — with 'wings', patches, streaks, quiffs, fronts, back, tips and tails to catch the eye	Until you brush or wash it out	You just take aim with an aerosol can — being careful to cover the eyes. If you want to tint after using an aerosol, make sure every trace is removed or the results could be dire!
Roughly speaking, piebald but it varies. A large range depending on the imagination and skill of the operator — and the time and money of the customer	Until regrowth and fading demand another expensive, but worthwhile session	Methods vary from salon to salon. 'Props' include a gun, silver foil, a selection of paintbrushes and a cardboard halo; only out of date salons use a bathing hat and a crochet hook. Takes forever to do . . . worth spending the time and money as the results are effective and flattering. PS Basically it's a bleach-and-tint job
Good quality henna will not only colour the hair but condition it too. Makes dull hair shiny and shiny hair lustrous	Practically forever — or at least until the roots show	With extreme caution and gradually. Don't try to be a redhead in one theatrical swoop. Don't use chemical henna over a tint — disaster will ensue, and your hair won't stand the strain
All-over colour — and the built-in conditioner adds sheen	Some last only until the next shampoo, some last for half a dozen	After shampoo. Press the button and the foam oozes out. Follow instructions about how long to leave it on
From subtle to startling — the all-over colour gives a 'hard shell' effect when it dries. Can also be used for streaking or tipping.	Washes out — but needs a strong shampoo, or two applications. Rinse WELL	After shampoo. Apply from tube and comb into style

▲ Achieved with something that looks like shaving cream and sounds like dessert. It's the new colouring mousse that sprays on in colours that range from subtle to wild. Just shampoo, wait a few minutes and rinse out.

▲ If it isn't a mousse it's probably a gel — today's way of adding colour and gleam to crisp, cropped hair. Can be used all over or here and there. Best when wet when it looks like father's brilliantine. When dry, the hair has a hard lacquered look.

TAKE A GIRL

How far should you go? As far as you like but it's generally considered more flattering to go lighter rather than darker. If this is your very first time round the colour circuit and you're less than a total extrovert, then it's probably wise to choose a shade not a million miles away from your own. Thanks to the excellence of today's colourants and the wide choice available the bolder ones among us can slide happily up or down the shade scale ignoring those who shout 'Danger!' if the move is more than one shade in either direction. If you do long to be more dramatically dark then a little caution is needed or there could be too great a contrast against your natural skin tones. And we do not all have it in us to look like a YOUNG Elizabeth Taylor. Generally, it's easier and more flattering to go lighter rather than darker. If you are a brunette who would prefer to live your life as a blonde, then all things are possible but your hair may first need to be 'lifted' (which is a euphemism for bleaching) before it is coloured so make sure it's in fine fettle before you start. And advice from an expert is always a good idea. As for blondes, natural, faded or mousy, the range of shades is mouthwatering and there are no holds barred as you choose from femme fatale platinum to country-girl corn gold. Redheads if they have any sense will thank their lucky stars and settle for a brightener or maybe a lightener.

All change

Whatever shade you are and whatever shade you choose, a change of make-up, no matter how subtle, will certainly be required. To prove the point our model tried out three different hair colours to see what happened to her skin tones and general colouring. Her own hair colour (in the centre picture) is a good rich brown. Her make-up is in shades of pink and brown with rosy lips. On the far left she has become a redhead with a tangerine tint to the mouth. Top left she's a warm chestnut and it's back to pinkish tones. Below left: paler brows and delicate pink lips . . . but still living proof that blonde can be beautiful — even for brunettes with a colour change in mind.

THE MULTI-TREND

The rainbow effects available today are brilliant enough to stop traffic — and often do! For every one who goes for all-over colour there are, perhaps, half a dozen who prefer to be streaked, marbled, tipped, highlit, lowlit, or just plain daubed with vastly differing shades. These are today's special techniques where, frankly, you need expert help for the best results. Once upon a more moderate time — some would even say boring — the colours on any one head ranged in shade from palest blonde to darkest brunette. Today the range can include rainbow hues that swap subtlety for a knockout effect visible from across the street. But the most popular multi-tones are anything from tortoiseshell to dappled sunlight and the gradations are achieved by bleaching and tinting streaks of hair in different shades to give half a dozen different tones on the one head. It takes quite a long time to do, involves wrapping sections of hair in foil squares and costs quite a lot of money. But it lasts for months and the regrowth is almost invisible. Sometimes the colour is painted on to the tips of the hair — which is quicker, cheaper, much more dramatic and can be done at home. Sometimes the colours are gentle — pink on blonde, gold on brown. Sometimes they're violent — emerald or royal or shocking pink. Subtle they're not. But fun they are.

▲ Black is beautiful — specially when it's streaked with flashes of royal blue to emphasize the subtle layering. The colour contrast gives a more textured look to straight hair and a simple head-hugging cut.

▲ Pink is pretty too, particularly when it's used to tip the edges of a precise blonde bob, cut to emphasize superb condition. Don't miss the pink accents on the cheekbones to echo the rosy glow.

◀ All the colours of the rainbow . . . and then some besides. To wrap each of the three shades in foil needs an expert hairdresser and an extremely patient client. The result: a head to turn other heads.

▲ Worth waiting for, worth paying for . . . a real colour knock-out with a red, white and black three-toned marbled effect that gives extra interest to the short and shaggy, layered cut.

▲ Some very unlikely pieces of equipment are used to get the special effects required from 'special techniques' popular today. This method is achieved with the acid of colour-coated corrugated paper 'sandwiches' clipped on to strands of hair. After half an hour, off they come and presto, the hair is a mass of blonded streaks. Other aids on the hair colouring scene include squares of aluminium foil and tiny 'bags' of clear plastic. These are used to isolate the strands and the finer the strands, the more subtle the effect, the more subtle the effect, the longer it takes and the more it costs. But generally agreed to be worth it . . .

▶ Dark roots are nothing short of desirable these days and here's a two-tone treat to prove it. The hair which started life as a brunette bursts out into a cascade of blonde 'tipping'. It relies on a knockout contrast of colour for the best, which means the most obvious, effect.

◀ If two-tone styles are fun, then three-tone styles are even more so. Especially if the contrasts are as exotic as this. Basic hair: blue-black. Accent colours: pink and gold. Fainthearts with nimble fingers can weave in the colour with false pieces. Others will need the expert aid of inspired stylists.

51

IT'S CRAZY!

For those who see no earthly reason why hair should be hair coloured, the world is going their way. The horizons that were once bounded on all sides by blonde, black, brown and red are now rainbow bright. A riotous choice of hair colours in shades that previously belonged only in the beauty and fashion worlds now offer something for every one of us in search of fun, fashion or fantasy. Or, come to think of it, all three simultaneously.

You have a hankering for hair to match your new pink pants? Why not! You feel royal blue is much more you? Blaze away! Emerald green, canary yellow, violent violet — they're all there at the squeeze of a tube, the stroke of a brush or the press of a spray. Out they come in a gush of lush colour that owes everything to creative imagination and technology and nothing at all to nature.

The best of today's wild and wonderful gels and mousses condition as they add instant drama to every shade of hair from the darkest to the lightest. Some disappear at the stroke of a well-wielded brush. Others last through half a dozen shampoos. So just make sure you really want to be a pink punk. You do? Then spray, gel or mousse away to your heart's content.

◄ Electric shock. Into the wild blue yonder with a puff ball of brilliance that owes its colour to a gel and its gravity-defying shape to a setting mousse that adds body and bounce.

▲ A tousle-haired fairy princess caught in a Force 9 gale, perhaps. But looking good as she peers through a sheer golden curtain of hair tipped with a sprinkling of fine fronds of brilliant pink, yellow and blue.

◄ Some of it's real hair. Some of it isn't. It's measured in feet rather than inches and all of it works together to make a cascade of red, white and blue. Patriotism was never like this. Eat your heart out, Lady Godiva.

▲ . . . Or would you, like your female forebears through the ages, rather be a blonde? Short and shaggy and high on touchability, a gleaming pom-pom of high carat gold with will-o'-the wisps out in front.

SPOT YOUR SHAPE

Shape, as we all know, is everything. Shape from the neck up is every bit as important as shape from the neck down. Clothes, cleverly cut and artfully arranged, can do a great deal for a girl who has a lot where she would like a little — and vice versa.

When it's shining bright and in peak, tiptop condition, hair can disguise, distract and flatter. It can even create its own optical illusions of perfection. It can broaden a brow, lessen a nose, round off the square and chop off an elongated chin. It can very definitely accentuate the positive — the bits we like — and eliminate the negative. It's absolute perfection we're seeking and why ever not? The oval-shaped face is considered to be as near perfect as makes

no difference these days so that's what most of us aim for.

In Shape

But first things first. Do you know for sure what shape your face actually is? A lot of us — most of us? — fail to see ourselves as others see us and are quite convinced we're totally square when in fact we're downright round.

To find out for sure, take a tip from the experts: Look at yourself in a good big mirror, take an old lipstick or eyeliner and draw the outline of your face on the glass. The evidence is there when you move away — and it very often comes as something of a surprise . . .

a Oval

b Long

c Square

d Round

e Heart

▲
The oval face fits in happily with almost any hairstyle. Here it looks its absolute prettiest with a softly brushed asymmetrical fringe (a).
A long face looks much less so with a fringe and well layered sides (b).
The square face is helped with a soft and definitely sideways movement (c).

A face that is a shade too round looks more angular and therefore more interesting with a skilful short, sharp crop (d).
The heart-shaped face is flattered and the wide brow disguised with a cascade of curls (e).

▲ If your face is *long* and your cheekbones high, a dramatically squared-off fringe will do what a good hairstyle should — accentuate the positive. Specially good for very dark hair.

▲ If you're the perfect *shape*, warmest congratulations. Whatever style you choose, don't clutter up that gentle chinline. Invest in an expert cut, dramatise the colour and keep all the volume up top where it will accentuate the highly desirable positive.

▶ A *square* face looks less so with an asymmetrical style. Needs plenty of volume and bounce to achieve its maximum effect so straight hair will need a soft perm.

SPOT YOUR SHAPE

If your hair is going to shape up to what's required of it as a flattering frame for your face, then it needs to be in peak condition. Which means it needs to be kept clean. Dirt and pollution in big cities are the major enemies, hotly followed — an apt description — by heated rollers and blow-dryers. If used too often these make even the best-tempered head of hair go its own unruly way. N.B. You CANNOT shampoo too often. You can, however, choose the wrong, too strong shampoo, use too much and rub too hard. With all these hazards behind you, you are about to embark on the adventure of a brand new style — the one that looked so wonderful on the beauteous model girl. You need more volume here or a touch of texture there? No problem. Today's colour and conditioning mousses will give all the extra body and bounce that you need. If your hair is straight and movement is your mood, then a light perm will do likewise. But most important of all is a good cut. Your friendly neighbourhood hairdresser, if well-trained (which is usually the case today), can persuade even the most recalcitrant hair to take on a new and more interesting life of its own. From then on it's up to you how it continues to shape up to requirements.

◄ If your face is *round*, you need height to deceive the eye of others. Best on strong, straight hair this style is layered in the front with the back hair bobbed just below the ears.

► A good style for a face that's *too square* — provided the hair is coarse and curly and there's lots of it. If not, then invest in a soft perm and always 'finger' it dry after shampooing.

◄ A cloud of gleaming black hair makes the perfect frame for a delicate *oval* face. If it's curly Afro type, you've a head-start. If not, then perm in the curls and allow it to dry naturally after washing.

► If your face is *oval* and your hair is fine and straight, this one's for you. Short, sharp and spiky it needs constant shampooing to keep it boyishly in shape. Contrast streaks and/or coloured tipping would add extra weight and volume to less than luxurious locks.

LONG IS LOVELY

From Rapunzel who let hers down to pull up a prince to Lady Godiva who did likewise for a complete cover-up job, long hair has always come in handy. As every man will tell you at the drop of a hairpin, it's extremely sexy and is said to be an open invitation for them to run through it barefoot. Be that as it may, long hair takes a lot of looking after if it is to look like silken strands rather than old rope. When you shampoo, apply a conditioner and leave on for a full minute. Then run your fingers through it several times before you rinse. Do NOT pull long hair when it's wet, so go carefully with that good coarse comb. Wet hair loses its elasticity and will break off. Such a pity when, as we all know, it takes forever to grow. (It just *seems* like forever — in reality it's a ½ inch a month.) Straight or curly, coarse or fine, long hair is well worth the time and trouble it undoubtedly takes to keep it in the pink. Or red. Or whatever colour it is that takes your fancy . . .

▲ A happy marriage of cut and subtle colour. The sides are layered and the natural waves are emphasised for extra movement. Very outdoorsy and very casual.

► The kind of hair that makes strong men weak and poets reach for their pen. After shampooing leave to dry in its own sweet way in order to preserve the pre-Raphaelite riot.

▲ For more sophisticated soirées, a more sophisticated look. The hair is wrapped round the head like silken skeins and fixed on high into a tiny topknot. The wayward wisp is fixed in place with gel.

▶ Take one shoulder-length mane of exuberant curls and persuade it into a new shape with a sprinkling of pretty blue bows fixed to some sturdy out-of-sight hairgrips.

SHORT IS SHARP

Short hair for girls is a comparatively modern innovation. It's not so long since the first flighty Twenties flapper flipped her lid and bobbed her hair. Then, while grandma quietly had the vapours, we had the shaven-necked shingle and the clipper-cut Eton crop. Between then and now, cutting hair has taken on the aura of an art form progressing from the short-back-and-sides snip in the female equivalent of the local barber shop to the point where hair stylists (as opposed to mere hair*dressers*) are stars in their own right. But let's give credit where credit's due. A skilled operator can work with hair in precisely the same way that a sculptor can work with clay, or a fashion designer with fabric. It's not just cut, it's positively caressed into shape — a little layering to build it up just here and a *soupçon* off the ends just there. The results of such selfless devotion to duty are young and bouncy styles which offer a girl a trouble-free life between trims which are usually needed about every month or six weeks.

Most short cuts need little or no life support systems — perms, rollers, etc. — but they do respond to frequent, gentle shampooing like flowers to the sunshine. Whether your hair is coarse and curly or fine and straight, there's certainly a short cut to make it look its very best — and thereby doing the same for you.

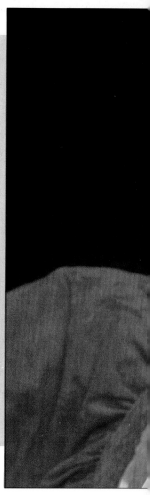

◄ When does short hair not look too short? When it's cleverly cut into layers that add extra volume that add extra flattery. Best for hair with a natural wave or a gentle perm.

► Straight hair that couldn't be straighter and wants to stay that way. A setting gel or styling mousse, used after shampooing, guarantees the desired spiky effect.

◀ A real sunburst of a style that wouldn't, couldn't, look as good in any other colour. If hair is going to be red, then there's a case to be made for going redder or even reddest.

▲ The interest is upfront and there's more than a touch of the Teddy Boy in the feathery quiff that lightly brushes the forehead before it disappears into a neatly layered bob at the back.

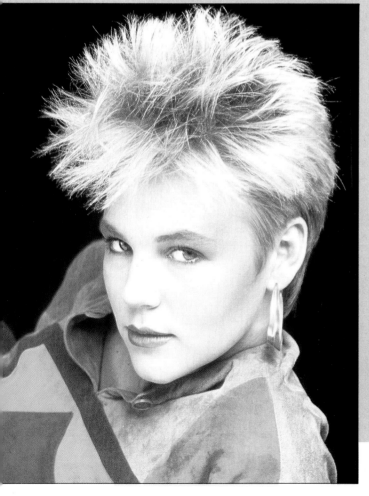

TAKE 2 GIRLS

So you've changed the colour of your hair and now want a change of make-up. The colour of your eyes, the colours you like to wear, the 'hot' favourite of the moment. . . all should influence your choice. But there are a few surefire winning combinations to keep in mind. The brunette with dark or hazel eyes should pick and choose among the cool and tawny tones. Any of the smoky blue or lavender eye colours, blended with a touch of brown or even soft purple. For lips, the bronze or copper colours or soft rose. All blondes should emphasise their fragility.

Keep lip colours in the pink rather than orange range and echo the eye's own colour with smoky blue or greenish shadow. A grey shadow with dark rosy lips is particularly good on blondes with silvery tones in their hair. Whether your hair is Afro or satin-smooth black, dark skin tones look best with eye and lip colours from the wine, purple or rosy brown range. Hit the colour highspots with the more vivid blues or greens teamed with hot pink lips. Redheads look their best in muted pink, grape or bronze lip colours with smoky blues or greens to match their eyes.

▶ The chestnut or mid-brown brunette with smoky 'blue' undertones in her hair colour can use pink, slate blue or lavender and purple shades for her eye make-up, and introduce wine and rosy red for both blushers and lips. Soft shades of blue both pale and dark also look wonderful as eye accent colours with dark brown hair and especially with blue eyes.

◄ On every blonde head of hair there are a thousand different shades. Blonde can be as bright as corn, as pale as champagne. As the light changes so the hair appears to change too. A golden glow for the blue-eyed blonde means smoky blue eye colours with accents of lavender and pink. A clear rosy red for the lips and just a touch of pink for the blusher. Apply all colour with the lightest touch since blondes need a minimum of vivid extras to complement their own delicate tones.

TAKE 2 GIRLS

▶ A new colour for your hair means a new colour for your face. Whether your hair is Afro black by nature or design, your choice includes all of the purple/pink/smoky-blue tones as well as the more subtle blend of wine/brown/pearl/sagey greens. And never forgetting, of course, that it's what you wear as well as the colour of your hair that sets the total tone.

◄ Nature may not have made you a redhead but then who actually needs Nature? What you will need is a whole new wardrobe of make-up colours specially designed to project the new and more colourful you. How about the fruity, flowery shades that combine violet, plum and raspberry tones for eyes, mouth and cheeks, for instance? Or steely blues and greens teamed up with clear ruby and wine reds.

COLOUR

YOUR CLOTHES

... While there is no-one to say you nay should you actually *wish* to paint your face blue, there are still a few justifiable rules in the world of beauty. In the wide-open world of fashion there is none. Wearing certain colours in certain ways, combining colours in pale or pulsating twosomes, threesomes or even foursomes is a fascinating way of expressing yourself, of communicating without words. Once you've learned the language of colour your wardrobe will work for you as never before.

Learn about the dark colours which recede and the pale ones which don't. Learn, too, about the 'speed' factor — orange registers fastest of all, then comes red, blue, black, green, yellow and violet with grey as the slowest, softest sell of all. Since none of us goes shopping nude with a cheque book or a credit card, there's a need for some judicious colour planning. Don't, however, get trapped in too rigid a plan that allows for no flights of colourful fancy. Cultivate a free spirit. Try out new combinations . . . primaries with primaries . . . pastels with pastels. Start with your basic backdrop and then use it as a launching pad for some colourful adventures . . .

SPOT-ON!

Every wardrobe worthy of its name needs a neutral or dark basic background against which to play the colour game. These are the working colours — black, white, grey, navy, brown, beige, burgundy, khaki. They can be used subtly with their own family of tones or boldly with unexpected contrasts. Or, as here, in made-for-each-other twosomes.

Some basics you just can't beat. Take black-and-white for a start. It goes anywhere, any time. Wear it for summer with black jeans and a sheer white shirt. Wear it in winter with a long black skirt, black boots and a huge white, woolly sweater. White silk with black cashmere... white satin with black velvet. Perfect partners at all times, black and white can make an intruder of any colourful addition. Seen here, black and white at its brilliant uninterrupted best. The dotty Dalmatian dress accessorised with nothing but black. Plus, of course, a friend of the family...

Turn the page for some further basic fashion philosophy...

BLACK MAGIC

Black is the number one basic that, more than any other, stays with us, season in and season out. It's a very grown-up colour which is why little girls long to wear it and any mother far-sighted enough to dress her 7-year-old in black velvet and white lace is likely to get her offspring's style buds off to an early start. Black frightens some tentative followers of fashion who see it as a demanding colour that looks good only on willowy blondes, flamboyant redheads or anyone who is svelte, sultry, soignée or just Spanish-looking. Not true. Black is prepared to be anyone's best friend — if you treat it right. Wear unrelieved black only if your skin colouring blooms without the help of too much make-up. (Or you're in mourning!) Whatever make-up you normally wear, in black you'll need more. Especially eyeshadows and blushers. Vivid red lips and nails to match punctuate black brilliantly. So do nudey pink ones — very sexy.

If black is your number one basic choice then there are two colourful paths to pursue. One is for extroverts and is enlivened with great splashes of brilliance — orange, red, blue, yellow, emerald, purple, shocking pink. Or travel the more subtle route with smoky or neutral tones — the spice colours, taupe, tan, slate, lavender. If maximum impact is your aim, invest in a huge multi-coloured shawl. Or wear a scarlet shirt and white satin tie with a businesslike black suit. Or an orange T-shirt, black jeans and a purple patent belt. Try an emerald heavy sweater with bold black and white check trousers. Wear all-black — including lacy tights — and spike with a pair of wicked red leather shoes. If you'd rather smoulder than burn then go for the laid-back look. Team your basic black with anything in leopard print. A T-shirt, even tights or, as seen here, a huge, leopard bag. And no basic black wardrobe is complete without the Little Black Dress — this one in jersey is teamed with black leather and beret. Other subtle partners: a Prof. Higgins cardi in lilac with just a touch of grey . . .

WHITE'S RIGHT

White stands for purity, virginity, fragility —
and fashionability. With white as your basic
shade you can straddle the seasons with
ease and, if you're not choosy, a large dry-
cleaning bill. Some whites, of course, are
washable so make a friend of those synthetics that blend with natural fibres and avoid
the more sleazy, easy-care nasties. White

looks warm and wonderful in the winter, cool and carefree in the summer. In sheer, see-through fabrics — lace, voile, pure silk — it exudes luxury and blatant sex appeal. In thick wool whether woven or handknit it can be as sporty and outdoorsy as any tough tweed. Above all, white is *flattering*. Ask any photographer who reflects white to light up a model's face. Or just wear a man-size white towelling robe over flesh pink. Yours. Seen here, other ways with white. Far left, fes-tooned with gold and silver glitter. Next, the outsize T-shirt which is to white what the Little Black Dress is to basic black — essen-tial. Below left, two ways with white and pastel. Last, white gets a touch of the primaries.

HOORAY FOR GREY

Black is black and white is white. Grey can be anywhere from the palest dove to the darkest charcoal. If you're choosing grey as your basic background colour, avoid extremes and go for the middle ground where a nice, friendly clerical grey will team happily with almost any shade you care to put its way.

Grey is a good mixer with both blatant brilliance or subfusc subtlety. But it is, above all, businesslike — hence the prototype man-in-the-grey-flannel-suit. Borrow it and then team it with a white T- or tailored shirt, black shoes and opaque black tights and you'll look every bit as corporate-minded. Bring the suit swinging out of the boardroom with witty flashes of colourful nonsense. A man-sized shirt in sugar pink, worn collar undone with a school-boy tie in acid yellow. Wear all-grey right down to nanny-type tights — and then add violent violet shoes. Like black, its sobersides second-cousin, grey needs dressing up not only with other colours but also with a rethink of your make-up. Wear grey and you need more colour in your face. Not necessarily bright or vivid colour but enough of it to make definite contrasts against your own skin tone. Lashings of grey eyeshadow in both pale and dark tones worn with a bronze lipstick and blusher look wonderful with grey, black and a touch of terracotta. Violet eyes, fuchsia lips and nails will spark up any shade of grey worn with any shade of pink.

Grey can spring sophisticated surprises when teamed with other basics; grey with dark brown — and add a drop of cream. Grey with black — plus a touch of palest lilac. Grey with navy — and a dash of scarlet. Seen here some Grade A grey ideas to point the way. Right, the basic grey indispensibles — a classic grey sweater and a sleeveless grey pinafore. Designed to live happily together or just as happily apart. Next, maximum sunshine on a rainy day — your basic grey partnered with rainbow bright hat, mac, umbrella and boots. Then a back-to-school grey with blazer and tie in a like-minded mood. And finally, another basic blend — grey with wine and black.

JOIN THE NAVY

Navy is for sailors, wearers of school uniforms and anyone who knows a basic fashion winner when they spot one. Navy can be darkly dramatic — and slightly surprising — as in a man's tuxedo in midnight blue which is just another name for navy. Or rough and tough as in a Guernsey sweater. There is British navy which is as dark as navy can go without turning black and there is French navy which is several tones lighter and considered to be easier to wear. Red, white and blue used to be more patriotic than fashionable until Chanel put them together for smart French ladies en route to the races. The same tricolor combo is still hard to beat but don't put them together in equal amounts or you'll look like the French flag. Try a navy suit, a white shirt with just the merest touch of red — a belt or a bag will do *tres bien*. Navy is a colour with such *sensible* associations. Think about navy satin for a dressy shirt with outsize smoky pearl buttons. Or a navy lace skirt worn with an emerald tunic loosely belted with rhinestone or tan leather rope. In the days when well-dressed women wore certain colours only at certain times of the year navy was *the* spring choice. It still looks wonderful in spring teamed with white and palest leaf green. Or curry and hot pink. It is equally comfortable in the winter with creamy cashmere or natural Aran knit. Wear navy in the summer heat with a tan and lots of gold hanging about your person. Wear navy in the autumn with heathery pink tweeds — and just a touch of ochre. Seen here four ways with navy. Far left, navy spiced with spice. Next, navy teamed with lilac, a hint of pink and a flash of red. Pictured, today's proof that white was, is and always will be navy's best friend. And finally evidence that blue-and-green should certainly be seen — with robust red.

BROWN STUDY

The first requirement of an adaptable basic is that it should be prepared to play both a leading and a supporting role. Which means that all basics, other than black and white, should be the most timeless and classic in their particular category. For instance navy rather than royal blue, clerical rather than dove grey. As each season's new favourites come and go these are the enduring ones that continue to act as a fashionable but neutral backdrop for the latest 'in' colour this time around.

If you've chosen brown as your basic, avoid the tan tones and go instead for a good dark brown — almost if not as dark as bitter chocolate. This is the brown that often looks its lively best teamed with the shades that are its first cousins in the family colour spectrum. These are all the orange/bronze/tawny tones usually associated with autumn. Which doesn't at all mean to say you should get stuck in the seasonal rut with brown or indeed any of the other best basics. Many fabrics nowadays have year-round potential. Heavy-duty brushed cotton, fine wool, denim, wool or cotton jersey enable you to take your favourite basic right through the four seasons with just a change of accessories. Dark brown jersey for instance looks sensational against a golden tan with nude pink lips and nails and lots of gold geegaws. A dark brown jersey skirt lights up a winter day when teamed with a cherry red heavyweight sweater. Brown and black spell unmistakeable sophistication. Try a brown handknit sweater with a black leather skirt. Or a black leather jacket over snuff brown trousers. With a cream shirt and a gold belt.

Brown is an outdoor colour as well as an indoor one. Outdoors it blends with its back-to-nature neighbours — slate grey, blossom pink and all the leaf greens from spring's palest to winter's darkest. Seen here, from left to far right: brown tone-on-tone from the darkest to the palest near-to-pink. Next, brown blossoms out in the company of pale pink and gentle green. Brown playing a supporting role to the primaries and finally brown partnered with orange and black. Brown is such an *adaptable* basic . . .

BEIGE RAGE

When is basic beige not basic beige? When it's blonde, bamboo, camel, fawn, straw, string, oatmeal or even porridge. Beige by any of these names looks expensive on blondes and ritzy on brunettes. Redheads should wear beige only if they have a creamy complexion rather than a pale pink one. Of all the basics, beige is the most self-effacing and needs to be handled with care and flair. Handle it well and it responds with a variety of moods that can't be beaten by any of its basic brethren. Or sisterthren.

One of the most successful ways to use beige is in the tone-to-tone register, building up through top-of-the-milk to camel. Very subtle. Very sexy. Splice it, perhaps, with just one hectic dash of coral pink. Lips and nails — or a vast sweater over a beige pleated skirt. With beige tights and shoes to match. And lots of pearls. Another word for beige is natural. Beige is what white is before it's bleached which may explain why beige and white is an unbeatable combination. Feminine, fragile, flattering. Think about a white cotton sweater, natural linen trousers and a black man-sized cardi. Beige is the ubiquitous basic that enjoys harmonious relationships with all the other basics. Wear it with black — and sugar pink. Or fuchsia. Wear it with grey and just a touch of burnt orange. Or with navy and flag red. Think about beige with dark brown and purple.

Seen here, three ways to go with beige as your basic. From right to far right: first all the beiges blended, tone-on-tone to look their ladylike best. Next, the classic camel topcoat in a vivacious mood sporting an earth-toned throw, an echoing touch of green in the shirt and a pair of singing scarlet trousers. Finally the classic camel topcoat teamed wtih an Aran sweater, dark brown trousers and just a touch of the blues. On the subject of vivacity, unless your colouring is as vibrant without make-up as it is with it, when you wear your basic beige, give yourself an extra boost with the blusher. And a shade more eyeshadow wouldn't go amiss either. To say nothing about lively lips and nails. A little extra time, a little extra trouble and you'll be a veritable beige rage . . .

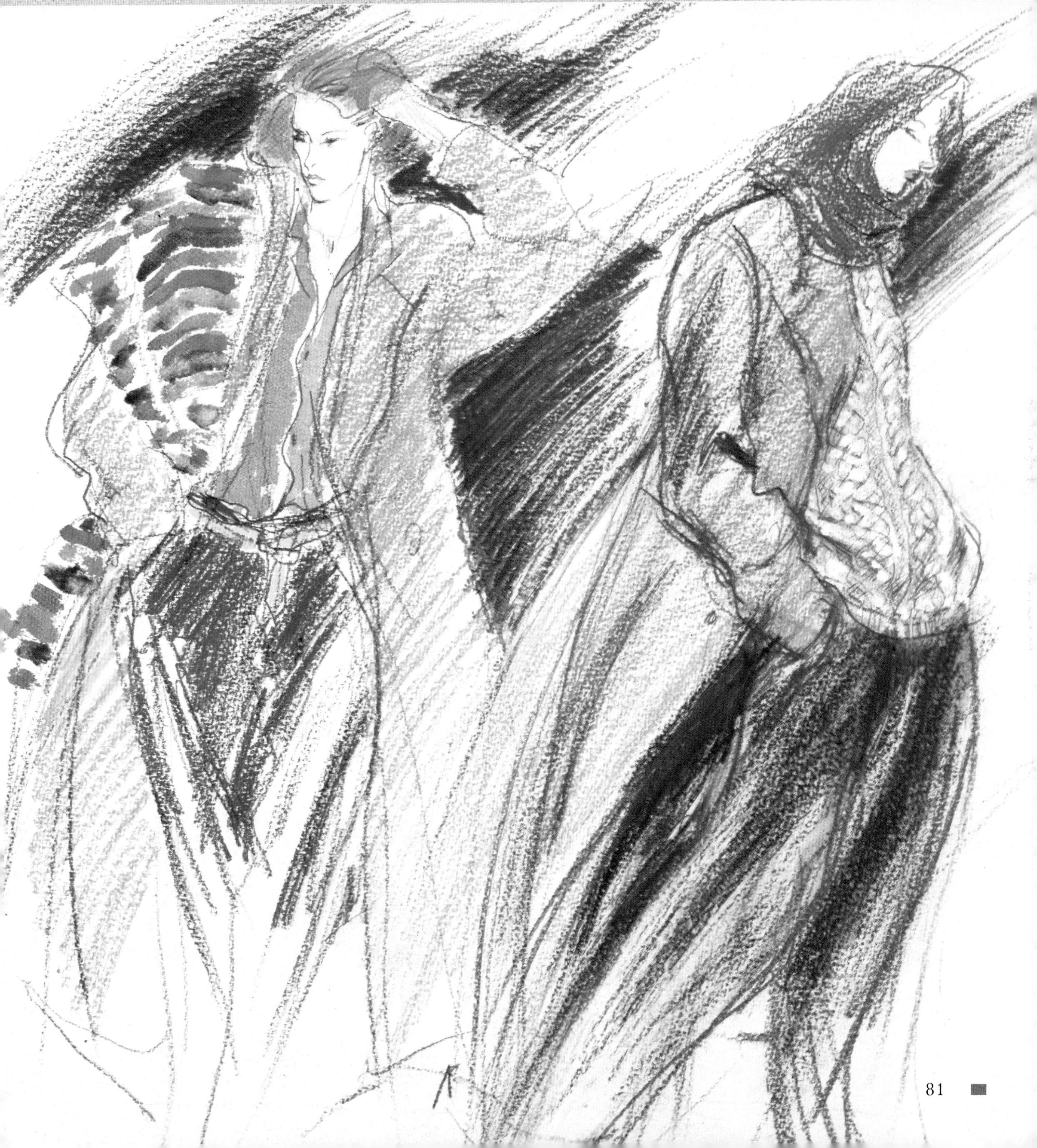

WINE AND ROSES

In its time it has been known as both wine and maroon but today it's very definitely burgundy and varies only marginally in its rich redness. Like its namesake, Burgundian wine, it sometimes has a discernible purplish hue. Other times there is a clear rosy glow. It's the colour of pomp and circumstance and royal robes and against a clear white complexion it is outrageously becoming.

Often easier to wear than the other traditional basics, burgundy is flattering to most complexions, making a fair skin look even fairer and a dark one more exotic. A burgundy-clad redhead with porcelain skintones and wine red lips and nails will look romantically pre-Raphaelite. Burgundy comes directly from the red spectrum and looks its becoming best with close and not so close members of its own tonal family. With fuchsia, with cerise, with rose pink, with grape and all the *vin rouges* now known as *ordinaire*. It's one of the 'warm' colours and responds well to shock tactics with make-up. If you're dark, try spearmint pink lips and nails and lavender eyeshadow. If you're fair try some bright orange lips and nails, with smoky wine eyeshadow and blusher. If burgundy is your basic choice go for the top-to-toe look — very Big City, very grown-up. Very glamorous. Apart from its red-to-pink partnerships, it responds to some more unusual liaisons. Try it with — a khaki sweater under a burgundy suit. With or without a pink muffler. Burgundy and dark olive green. Burgundy and steely blue. Burgundy with acid-yellow and navy.

From far left to far right, first, burgundy with a boldly checked beige and dark blue sweater. Next, a burgundy top joins the navy and adds a flash of red and a dash of bright yellow at foot level. Then the burgundy basic — matching sweater and skirt and, finally, burgundy separates get together with a classic topcoat in clerical grey. Added attractions — the pale beige muffler and black gloves. Out of sight — black tights and black shoes. Very classy. Very vintage.

TRAD TRENCH

▲ The trench coat as we have come to know and love it — tough and countrified and exuding well-bred classic confidence. It's best-dressed country cousins include bulky handknit sweaters, cashmere scarves, Prof. Higgins' hats. Other naturals — **above**: a huntin' shootin' fishin' type bag; and **far right** (top to bottom): a tan leather waistcoat worn *over* the coat, bold argyll check socks and, new to the country scene, baggy brown trousers worn at half mast.

They're like your best friend — the one you can take anywhere. One day they're stomping about the countryside and the next they're out on the town. And they're equally at home morning, noon or dressed-up night. They are the colour chameleons that rate a place in every well-planned wardrobe because they can change their role according to the time, the place and the mood of the moment.

Take the trad trench coat for starters. For years its natural habitat was always the countryside where it still looks wonderful accessorised with tweedy textures in creamy, earthy colours — not forgetting, of course, the famous green boots. But in today's exciting world where rules do *not* rule OK the trench coat is a real go-anywhere treasure. Tart it up with city chic and it can play any role you choose to give it. Breaking away from the countryside palette it looks frankly sensational teamed with scarlet, totally dramatic with black and makes the perfect foil for flashes of brilliant pink or emerald green.

From now on any self-respecting trench coat should lead at the very least a double life.

◄ The trench coat on the town. **Right**: swaggering over a jaunty red dress with a flashy patterned shawl; **below left**: complementing a black tuxedo; and **below**: punctuated with vivid accessories plus a glimpse of its own checkered lining.

SINGIN' THE BLUES

Blue denim is to Twentieth Century Woman what the fig leaf was to Eve: her most indispensible cover-up. Invented in France nearly 100 years ago, it has transcended every fashion limitation known to a rough, tough heavy-duty working fabric.

Today, thanks to a world-wide fashion industry that can spot a good idea when it sees one, blue denim is available in every hue from stone-washed pale to all-but-black. And equally good worn either with traditional hoedown check shirts and howdy-pardner boots, or gussied up with rhinestones, gold or lashings of lace. It knows no barriers of age or class and can look good on everyone from the youngest to the oldest, from the smallest to the tallest, the blondest to the darkest.

Pick denim and you've got yourself the perfect partner for any colour games you want to play. If it's subtlety you're after then team it up with tobacco brown or black. If you'd like it a touch less butch wear it with pastel pink or baby blue or anything in white as long as it's frilly. For maximum impact team it boldly with the primaries — especially its soulmate, flag-waving red. And remember: there's nowhere denim can't go, nowhere it won't look good, from decorating the back of a 1000cc Kawasaki to a high-life ritzy cocktail stool.

Your merest fashion wish is blue denim's most urgent command.

▼ **Below left**: the broad belt of many colours. **Right**: the classic denim twosome, jeans and bomber jacket, prettied up with silver beads and bracelet plus a flash of turquoise from the hanky pocket.

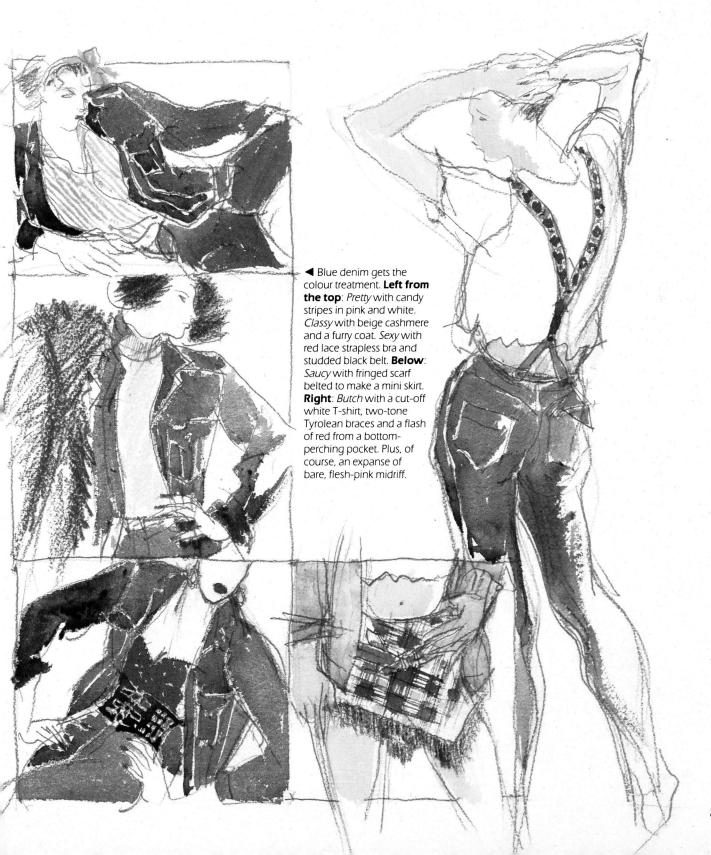

◀ Blue denim gets the colour treatment. **Left from the top**: *Pretty* with candy stripes in pink and white. *Classy* with beige cashmere and a furry coat. *Sexy* with red lace strapless bra and studded black belt. **Below**: *Saucy* with fringed scarf belted to make a mini skirt. **Right**: *Butch* with a cut-off white T-shirt, two-tone Tyrolean braces and a flash of red from a bottom-perching pocket. Plus, of course, an expanse of bare, flesh-pink midriff.

A JUMP AHEAD

In its time it has had several names. It used to be a siren suit. Or a boiler suit. Today it's a jump suit. Whatever you call it it's the front-buttoning one piece garment that is as short on shape as it is high on style.

Made in every fabric from creased cotton to silk jersey it transcends seasons and time of day. It can be cheap and cheerful or expensive and elegant but whatever the price tag it will be the most versatile occupant of most wardrobes. For maximum adaptability choose a neutral shade and experiment with a varied palette of secondary colours to change its shape as well as its mood. Worn baggy and boyish with bright accessories it starts the day in casual style. Later on, loaded down with subtly shaded extras it takes on a whole new personality.

Wherever it goes, the jump suit is fun and it likes its share of jokey accessories — the outsize bags and baubles, the borrowed-from-the-boys boots and caps, the flash of brilliant colour peeping provocatively out, its voluminous bulk grabbed into a broad belt. And talking of bulk, don't forget to buy it at least one size larger than you think you need. In the world of the jump suit big is beautiful.

▼ The jump suit and colourful friends. **Far left**: two blues with a twist of magenta at the neck. **Left**: outlook pale and interesting with a single flash of brilliant orange. **Below**: with a broad belt at the waist. And at foot level maximum impact socks checked in two-tone green with flat black boots or lace-up running shoes.

◀ Start with a jump suit and move smartly into colour. **Left, from the top**: a bulky grey blouson and red muffler. Open-necked with a striped T-shirt in fuchsia and white. Evening glitter with an Ecru lace camisole top and a gold knitted sweater tied loosely round the hips. **Right**: evening glamour with a black tuxedo jacket and black satin cummerbund. Essential extras — jumbo-sized rhinestone earrings and a multi-strand rhinestone necklace. Final black accent — a pair of dainty black high or medium heeled pumps.

THE SKIN GAME

Black leather has come a long way since it first leapt off the back of a beatnik's motor bike. Nothing in any well-stocked wardrobe today is more versatile or more acceptable on any scene than black leather which has somehow managed to slough off its sinister image while clinging cleverly to its innate sexiness.

Whether it's as thick as tweed or as supple as silk it's a natural for good styling, and there's hardly a colour or texture it can't partner with effect. With sweaters, tweeds and sensible shoes it reeks of daytime respectability. Comes the evening and it swings into style with some unexpected liaisons of colour and texture, like cream lace or gleaming red satin. It hasn't, however, deserted its original loyal friends and still looks good with metal studs and a sharp white shirt.

Anyone with an interest in today's fashion scene should have at least *one* black leather number in their wardrobe. If not, you risk a black mark . . .

▼ **Below**: black leather enters the primaries. The briefest of miniskirts worn with the biggest of sweaters in the brightest of blues. A yellow scarf at one end and emerald green legs at the other.

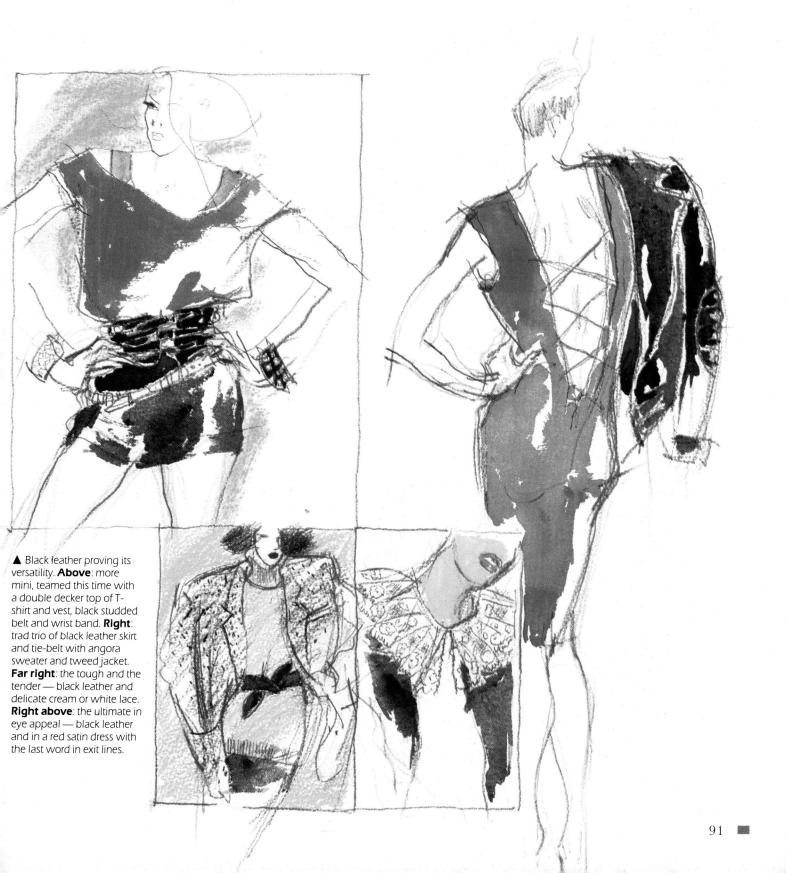

▲ Black leather proving its versatility. **Above**: more mini, teamed this time with a double decker top of T-shirt and vest, black studded belt and wrist band. **Right**: trad trio of black leather skirt and tie-belt with angora sweater and tweed jacket. **Far right**: the tough and the tender — black leather and delicate cream or white lace. **Right above**: the ultimate in eye appeal — black leather and in a red satin dress with the last word in exit lines.

COLOUR RULES O.K.

Open your wardrobe door. How many colours do you see there? One (comparatively) well-dressed girl about town confessed that her collection of fashionable outfits, new, old and all stations in between reminds her each morning of porridge. It's true she has a reputation as a restrained dresser but what a lot of fun she is missing.

The neutral shades do, of course, have a properly respected place in the fashionable scheme of things but can be deadly boring if not spiced up from time to time with blasts from a more vibrant palette. Beige for a start looks its muted best accented with denim blue. Or paprika. Or both together. Brown looks less sombre touched with rose pink. Or pillar-box red. Or, again, all three together — plus, perhaps, one note of summer-sky blue. Grey goes well with terracotta and just a hint of purple. Once you're in a colourful frame of mind the permutations are virtually endless.

The one rule to remember is that there are positively and absolutely *no* rules to inhibit anyone in search of a more colourful outlook. Red-and-green-should-never-be-seen may have been a favourite chant of grandmama and likewise black-and-brown-will-make-you-frown. They may have made *her* frown but for us in today's dare-to-do-it world there are no discordant combinations to be dismissed without trying, and no illicit liaisons. Fuchsia and scarlet? Magenta and purple? Acid yellow and marigold? If nature can make them look wonderful side by side in a colourful garden, you can do it too.

Use your eyes

With all the world to choose from how do you home in on those colours that are right for you? Your best ally is your eye — but don't waste money on expensive mistakes. Experiment wtih scarves, ribbons, cheapo T-shirts. Hold them up to your face to see how they affect your skin tones which for all of us are basically blue or yellow. Or, if that idea alarms you, pink or peach. The blue/pink group will always look best in cooler tones while the yellow/peach group should choose warmer ones.

CLASH WITH DASH

There comes a moment in every girl's life when the safe colours that may well be her usual choice will simply not do. She's in a mood to break out into something wild and wonderful and why not? Colour, lots of it, is what her heart desires and what her heart should get since colour, as we all know, is a great antidote to gloom.

Colour, boldly worn, has a way of making us not only look good but feel that way too. Slip into a vast crimson sweater and/or don a pair of royal blue tights and suddenly on a cold grey winter morning your smile is readier and your step is springier. Think pink and team it with grapefruit yellow and the summer sunshine is even sunnier. Operate on the basis that two bright colours are minimal, three are that much better and four can be nothing short of sensational. Remember, too, that a clash has dash and to mix is often better than to match. We live in the age of stunning separates which means that tops and bottoms can be permutated in a million mouth-watering ways, layering on your colours as you go. The more the merrier, the brighter the better. Try a T-shirt in yellow over a vest in violet teamed with emerald tights. Or put a blue with red with pink. Or orange with turquoise with lime. Punctuate your point with equally brilliant caps, hats, scarves, shoes, boots, belts and bejewelled bits and bobs that beckon us in the clear-cut tones that used to exist only in paintboxes.

Colour codes

And as you pick and choose among the primaries you might like to ponder the inner meaning of every colour that tempts us: red means virility and love; green stands for hope and tranquillity; pink is romantic and brown workaholic; orange is generous, violet is mystical, yellow is extrovert. Turquoise has inner strength and blue is feminine which must surely confuse a lot of boy babies.

The message is clear: if you fancy a colour don't fight it. Merely remember that brighter clothes need brighter faces so just adjust your make-up and follow your fancy. It's more fun in colour.

IN TONE, IN TOUCH

In fashion as in music there are interesting discords as well as subtle harmonies. Crescendos alongside diminuendos. A well-planned wardrobe needs a bit of both. Loud, bright primaries provide maximum volume. More subtle sounds come from mixing tone with tone. If, for instance, brown is your basic choice, then complement it with the nearby earthy tones — terracotta, top of the milk, butter, cream. Navy tone-on-tone takes in slate, palest grey — even black. Green tones include palest bud to darkest leaf. Khaki tones and teams with olive and lemon. Wine blends absolutely perfectly with all the rosy pinks right down to *bois de rose*.

Stay close to your basic shade, accent it within its own family and you could come up with a veritable tone poem. (And remember to keep your make-up colours — particularly your eye shadows close to home, too.) But don't mix only tones, play tricks with textures as well. Mix silk-smooth suede with coarse handknits, leather with the shiniest satin, denim with starched white frills, heavy-duty tweed with chiffon. Be clever with your clothes as you stir the fashion pot — and come up with some exciting new combinations.

◀ Tone on tone — texture on texture. The colour mix: brown, cream, natural, butter, conker. The texture mix: suede, cashmere, handknit, cotton, lambswool, leather. The effect: perfect harmony — specially with make-up in the same rosy register.

▶ A real rule-breaker, a real stunner. Take one huge Aran sweater. Team it, perversely, with a froth of a skirt in the finest black lace. Pile on the rhinestones, slide into black lace tights and prove the undoubted attraction of opposites.

PATTERN ON PATTERN

If there's one phrase in fashion that ought to be banished it's the one that suggests that something or other doesn't 'go with' something else. In today's fashion world where freedom reigns anything can 'go with' absolutely anything provided it's done with dash. Like love and marriage and horse and carriage, pattern happily goes with pattern

regardless of look, weight or feel. Whether they're woven or printed, small scale or large, most patterns fall into clearly defined groups. To mix a star performer from one group with a star performer from another used to be the fashion equivalent of mixing oil with water. You shouldn't and couldn't. In today's colourful scene different patterns not only mix but positively wallow in each other's company. Spots sit well with stripes, checks go with either or both. Tartan looks terrific against a splash of flower power and flowers bloom against spots which just about brings us back to where we came in.

Make pattern on pattern work for you: wear a bright flowered shawl over a sober check; a print dress with patterned tights; a red and white polka dot bow tie, a pink striped shirt and a navy pin-stripe suit. Or how about a fair isle sweater, a bold checked shirt and a striped scarf? Imagination is the name of this game and the more patterns, the more points. Any number can play . . .

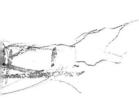

◄ The wow factor! Add pattern to pattern for maximum impact. **Far left**: flower power co-habits with animal prints. **Left**: who's afraid of the big, bold check? Not you as you add both stripes and a dash of print. **Right**: an exuberant collision of colour and pattern. Two different tartans team up with a romantic flower print. And don't miss the vivid accessories — as if you could! Total result: sizzling.

SHAPING UP

First things first. This is *not* about height. It's about shape, so whether you're towering or tiny forget about your extra inches or lack of them and concentrate instead on getting in shape with diet, discipline or dancing. If the results, perish the thought, are less than perfect, there are plenty of tricks to play to deceive the eye.

Clever deceivers

If you're top heavy choose separates with the darker colour at the top. Wear big shawls, padded shoulders, dolman sleeves. Avoid clinging fabrics, a close fit, and breast pockets. Hips wider than you'd like? Draw attention elsewhere with brightly coloured sweaters, padded shoulders, interesting tops and tunics in light bright colours. Thick waist? Avoid anything too fitted and always wear your belts low-slung round the hips. Combat jackets look good as do baggy sweaters.

Anyone with figure problems below waist level should attract attention higher up with scarves, big earrings and busy necklines. If your legs stop too soon elongate them in the eye of the beholder with tights and shoes to match or tone with each other and/or the outfit you're wearing. Your bottom's bottoming out? Wear generous skirts and floaty fabrics or long, loose tunic tops. And whether your problem is too much or too little, remember that loose is lovely, tight is terrible and a figure-hugging fit flatters no-one who isn't perfect. Other points to ponder upon: dark shades retreat, light ones advance. Vertical stripes slim and elongate, horizontal ones broaden and shorten. For more deceits, turn the page . . .

Take 2 girls

On the right, two attractive and successful model girls with a 10-inch differential in their height prove that it's only shape that counts. They're both wearing the current version of that hardy perennial, the safari look.

The fashion plan for both girls is identical and with identically flattering results. No concessions to their different heights at all. None is needed.

THINK PINK

If you want to go unnoticed in a crowd, don't wear pink. Pink is a magnet, attracting attention, demanding admiration. Pink is the colour with outrageous sex-appeal that manifests itself the moment a new-born baby girl is giftwrapped in that ooh-aah sugar almond shade. Experts who study the psychology of colours confirm that pink in its paler reaches is romantic and soft with an image of intimacy. More aggressive pinks like shocking and fuchsia send out more assertive messages with the same inbuilt sexuality.

Pinks, in all shades from naughty nude to mischievous magenta adjust happily to both winter and summer living. Vivid cerise can be a real beach belle — especially with swimsuit and sunspecs to match, and a pink frilly dress will make its wearer the life and soul of any winter party.

If you really want to be in the pink . . . think pink.

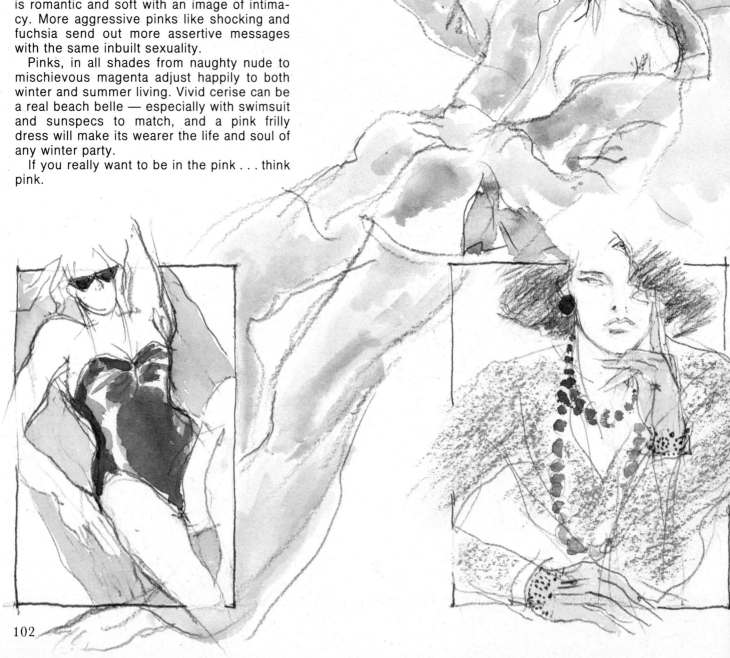

◄ Thinking pink? **Far left**: wear it on the beach and be the brightest pebble around. Best, of course, with a touch of tan. **Left**: once in her lifetime every girl ought to own a pair of pink satin pyjamas — and sash them in limpid lavender silk. **Left below**: partner pale pink with bright pink and spike with grapefruit yellow. **Below**: add a touch of pink frivolity to a sobersides dark suit. **Right**: pink in its most come-hither mood, partnered with black lace and a bowled-over male admirer.

BOLD GOLD

Gold is precious. Gold is gorgeous. Gold has unmistakable come-hither charms and deserves to be worn wth flamboyant flair by ritzy redheads, bold blondes or darkly dramatic brunettes. Gold, previously a regal pomp-and-circumstance shade has now found its place among the wearable fun and fantasy on today's fashion scene. Real cloth-of-gold may have weighed Majesty down but we can lightheartedly enjoy the suppleness of golden leather, lame and Lurex.

Gold was once a very strictly nocturnal prowler appearing resplendent at balls and other after-dark happenings. Today it's geared up to go anywhere, any time. (Quiet good taste, it isn't.) Gold can be worn in modest quantities — baubles, bangles, beads, belts or boots. Or even more modestly as metallic touches for eyeshadows, on fingernails or lips. Bold gold in a great shimmering swathe makes a wonderful skinny mini, a sensational shirt or a day-for-night hold-everything handbag. Gold is the perfect partner for brown, for grey, for sand, for khaki. With white it looks wonderfully Grecian goddess. With black it looks rich and only marginally vulgar. Certainly not enough to worry about . . .

◄ Bold, go-anywhere gold galore sending out its unmistakeable come-hither message. **Far left**: glistening on the beach, golden bikini pants with a camouflage bandana top. **Centre**: the lure of a lamé shirt teamed with an animal print vest and film-director jodhpurs. A business-like brown belt and — why not? — gleaming gold boots. **Below left**: the shining vastness of a golden shoulder-slung holdall; and, **below**: a plain neckline brightened up with a swathe of golden mesh. **Right**: gold at its boldest and no-holds-barred best: a slinky mini and a white strapless top. The jacket — a furry fake stencilled with golden spots. An outfit with the golden touch guaranteed to annihilate the competition.

SEEING RED

Red is the colour that sings out loudest across a crowded room. Its come-hither message is unmissable, so don't wear red if you don't mean it. Whether you choose to wear red from head to toe, in total or in touches, on top or underneath, red has strongly sexual vibrations that vary in meaning according to the fabric used. Red satin is for sultry sirens, red flannel is saucy, red velvet is sensual and red leather is seductive. (Red cotton confuses and doesn't count!)

Red is the colour of heat, capable of stirring emotions to boiling point. But red, paradoxically, is a winner in the summer worn against a golden tan. And bright red lips. Red is a wonderful winter brightener adding cheerful grace notes to otherwise sombre outfits. A scarlet scarf with black, a vermilion sweater with bitter chocolate brown, flag red with olive green or khaki. For more flamboyant liaisons try red with shocking pink, saffron or kingfisher blue. And no wardrobe is complete without at least one pair of bright red shoes. To be worn, of course, with black tights in true come-hither tradition.

◄ Red hot reds. **Far left**: red goes to the head with sooty eyes signalling from behind a wicked red veil. **Left**: red at its reddest against nude skin pink with *Gilda* gloves for peeling off. **Below left**: a scarlet belt of corset proportions to cinch the waist and cause comment. **Below**: red for lovely lace-clad legs and flirty feet. **Right**: red sizzling away where only you and yours will know about it. Hers: vest and bikini pants with a towel to tone. His: cotton printed and boxer shaped.

BLACK LOOKS

Of all the come-hither colours, black is the most chameleon in its sex appeal. It can be all things to all women — and men. It can be demure as in the ubiquitous Little Black Dress that clings with subtle suggestiveness to otherwise unsuspected curves. It can hit the heights of drama in black satin, skin-tight and preferably slit to the thigh. Black is romantic in lace, voluptuous in velvet, and black fishnet tights as every fancy dresser will confirm are terribly tarty. And then there's the most sensational black stunner of all — the sophisticated 'smoking' that has never looked as good on a man since Marlene Dietrich made it her own. The paradox of this most masculine of modes making a female look her feminine best is something to ponder upon, be grateful for and, having done so, start saving up to buy one.

Question: can anyone wear black regardless of hair colour or skin tone? Answer: yes to hair. But reappraise your makeup and veer towards brighter or more positive colours and be prepared for a repaint or repair job halfway through any evening. Or you may be signalling go forth rather than come hither . . . .

◄ Black looks. **Far left**: Black and white accented with red braces hanging provocatively about. **Left**: a dream of a dress in satin and lace. **Left below**: jet beads sparkle blackly on a man-sized cardi. **Below**: timeless black magic lacy legs and stiletto heels. **Right**: black at its most sophisticated — the 'Smoking' worn with nothing between you and the strictly tailored jacket. This 'Smoking' has a skirt to show off sheer black-clad legs with high heeled teeter-totter shoes.

A COLOUR P.S.

By now you should be thinking colourful thoughts, full of enthusiasm about wonderful new ways to wear wonderful new colour combinations. How will scarlet look with my basic brown? Does orange look O.K. with navy? What about pink with khaki? Whatever the basic shade in your wardrobe there will be an infinite variety of twosomes, threesomes or even foursomes that are stunning to look at and fun to wear. Seen here in your at-a-glance guide are just a few for starters. Try them out and gain yourself a reputation for being somewhat of a wiz with colour. But then that was always the idea, wasn't it?

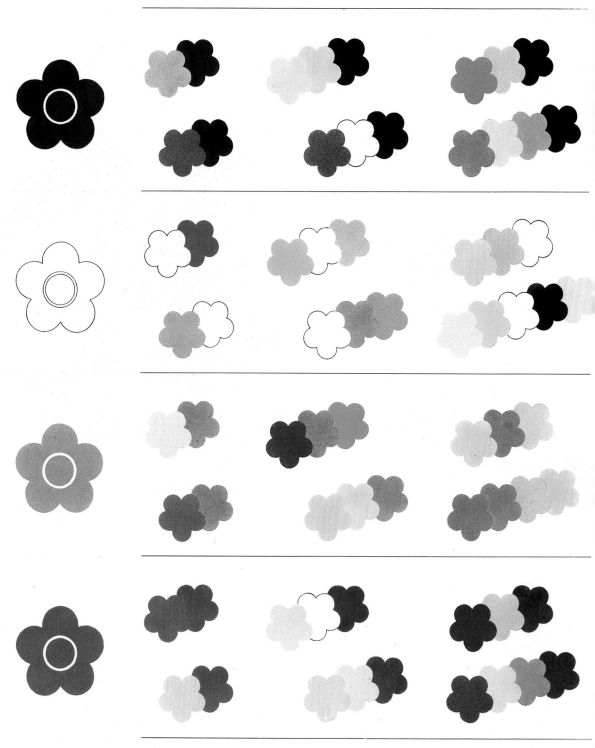

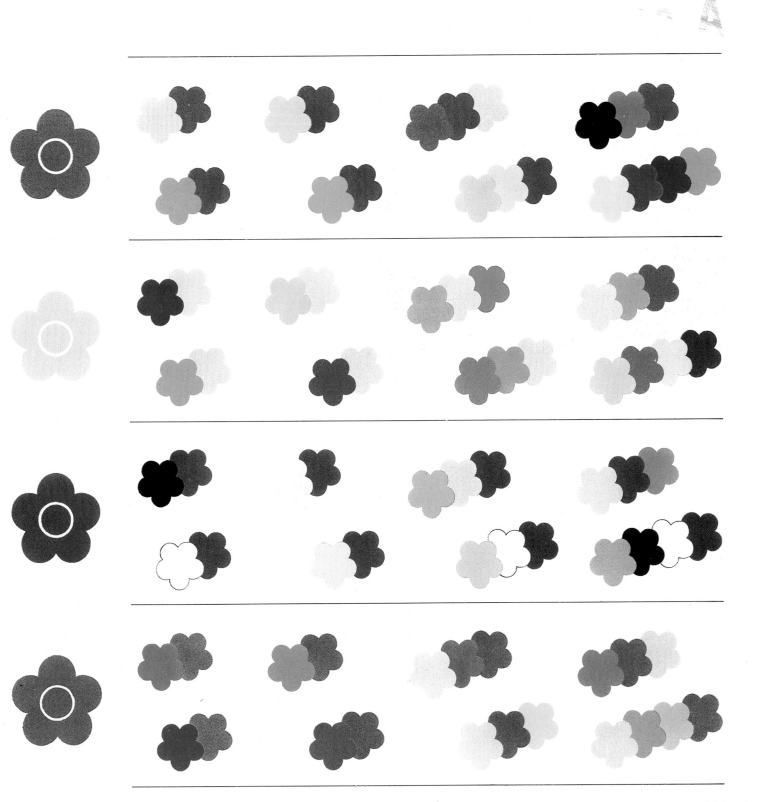

ACKNOWLEDGMENTS

The publishers would like to thank the following people who contributed greatly to *Colour By Quant.*

In addition to Mary, the following members of Mary Quant Limited were very actively involved in the planning of the book:

Alexander Plunket Greene
Elke Hundertmark
Mary-Ellen Lamb (make-up consultant)
Ursula Hudson (fashion consultant)

MARY QUANT ♣ (Trademarks of Mary Quant Limited)

Generous assistance was also provided by the following:

Ian Hutchinson, photo session manager
Theresa Fairminer, make-up on pages 84-101, 102, 109
Aitch from Vidal Sassoon, hair stylist on pages 70-101, 102-109
Bill Reed, styling for page 8 bottom, 9 top, bottom right, 11 top right
Ursula Hudson, styling for all photography, except above
Sally Parkes and Mark Betty, who assisted Ursula Hudson
Sheila Chandra, singer, model for top left photograph page 11
Izzy Bricknall, fashion illustrator's model
Kai Choi, glossary illustration
Hanife Hassan, illustrations pages 32-39
Yvonne Binns-Shaw, illustrations pages 30, 92-93

The following companies kindly contributed clothes for fashion photography:

Acquascutum
Rita Brown
Bernstock and Spiers
Browns
Butler and Wilson
Crolla
Sarah Dallas
Detail
Edina and Lena
Fiorucci
Flip
Ellis Flyte
Rider Footwear
Michaela Frey
Maude Frizon
Katherine Hamnett
Robin Higdon
Margaret Howell
Kenzo
Lonsdale Sports
Mulberry Company
Plantation
Patricia Roberts
Susan Wainwright
Daniel Watkins
Wendys Stall Kensington Market

The following organizations and individuals gave kind permission to reproduce the pictures in this book:

Daniel Galvin 48 right, 51 below, 55 above right, 58-59, 59 above, 61; L'Oreal 45 above, 55 below, 56 below left, 59 below; Vidal Sassoon 43, 49, 50, 50-51, 51 above, 53 left, 55 above left, 56 above, 58 left, 60-61; Shumi 48 left, 52-53 right; Trevor Sorbie 56 below right, 57, 60; Toni and Guy 45 centre and below; James Wormseer 4